Guitar For Begir

CW00497154

The Ultimate Guide to Learning Guitar and Mastering Guitar Basics, with Chords and Strumming Exercises for Best Results

Nicolas Knoll

Copyright © 2015, All Rights Reserved

Table of Contents

Introduction 4

About the Author 6

Chapter 1 - Guitars 101 and the Mindset...9

Most common guitar types 9

How to choose the best first guitar 13

Necessary mindset - how to practice, reach your goals, and not give up 18

Guitar parts explained 25

Essential guitar accessories 29

Chapter 2 - Getting started 36

Understanding The Note circle 36

Guitar tuning and names of the open strings 38

How to find and remember any note anywhere on a guitar fretboard 39

How to read tablature..44

Finger names and how to read chord boxes...47

Pick versus fingers, and how to hold a guitar pick properly 48

How to hold a guitar and correct body posture..53

Chapter 3 - Learning guitar chords 55

3 main types of chords 55

Basic Minor Chords..58

Basic Major Chords..61

Basic Dominant 7th Chords 67

Introduction to barre chords 74

Finger strength and stretching exercises 80

Best exercise to master the chord changes..86

Chapter 4 - Working on your strumming skills...89

Understanding time signatures 89

How to strum a guitar..89

  6 strumming patterns 95

  Why you should use metronome in your practice 99

  More ways to develop great rhythm.................................... 100

Where to next? 104

Conclusion 106

Check out my other books... 107

Introduction

After all the years I've spent learning, practicing and playing guitar I strongly believe that learning how to play this wonderful instrument can transform and enrich your life like you never thought was possible! If you decided to embark upon this miraculous journey, full of beauty, and new discoveries, then I can truly congratulate you, and say that it's an honor being able to help you learn guitar with this book!

This is a never ending journey. The process of learning to play music on any instrument never stops. Along the way you'll find that the more you learn, the more there is to learn. The truth is, you will never be able to learn everything. Even a guitar legend like Tommy Emmanuel, who plays for over 55 years, says that he still learns new things almost every day. The secret (and the point of all this) is to be able to enjoy the journey, enjoy the process of learning, and enjoy playing; get the most out of it since you'll never be able to learn everything anyway (nor will you want to). :)

By learning guitar and getting into the world of music, and maybe even creating a music of your own (there is music within all of us and we can all tap into it), you can become a better version of yourself - more intelligent, creative and confident person. You'll definitely be proud on yourself. It's such an accomplishment! I'm speaking from experience and from what I've seen happen to others who started playing guitar and decided to stick with it.

The purpose of this book is to lay out the foundations that you will need to learn and master in order to reach that level from which you can build upon and further develop your guitar skills, and your skills as a musician as well. You have probably heard of the house analogy: If you don't have a proper foundation set, everything you build upon later is going to eventually collapse.

That's why you need a strong foundation. Many people find this out the hard way and give up too early because they struggle with learning something that is way beyond their skill level. They haven't spent enough time mastering all the necessary foundational skills. There are other factors for giving up like: lack of motivation, negative beliefs and self-talk, being impatient and focusing too much on the end result...

If you think that you're not talented enough, I want to show and convince you that anyone, and I really mean **anyone**, can learn to play guitar, have as much fun as possible and express him/herself to the point of tears and/or profound joy. With this book I want to help you master the foundations by explaining the most important concepts that an aspiring guitarist needs to know, and what he/she needs to work on right from the beginning in order to achieve his/hers goals on guitar, no matter how small or big they are. In that regard, I'm also going to give you some of the best exercises for developing certain skills, like chord changing and strumming, and show you in detail how to practice them and even make up your own exercises.

This book is aimed for:

- People who are thinking about buying and learning guitar
- Beginners who are completely new to guitar
- Guitar players and beginners who have already played for some time but are struggling
- Anyone who would like to go through the basics, solidify them and maybe learn something new (I share some awesome tips and exercises that are not common knowledge.

Before I forget, I wanted to mention that when you buy this paperback version of the book you can also get the Kindle version for free! It contains some useful links that I cannot put here for obvious reasons. :)

Now let's get started. Enjoy learning!

About the Author

- First of all, who am I and why should you follow my advice?

My name is Nicolas, I've been playing guitar constantly for almost 10 years now, and I must say - what a wonderful and rewarding journey it has been! I wanted to share with you some of my back-story as it can benefit you.

I was always fascinated by guitar players. As a teenager I always watched in awe when someone played, and I admired their ability to evoke emotions in people who were listening to their playing. In any social circumstance that I took part in, it was always fun having a guitar around and someone who can play. I always wanted to be that person - the one who plays guitar.

I must admit, I started playing for all the "wrong" reasons. I was a naive 15-year-old with confidence issues. What inspired me the most to start learning guitar was being popular amongst friends and certain girl(s). What happened soon after I started was something that completely changed my world and my perspective. I discovered a new passion in life - music and playing guitar, and I was so much more immersed into learning how to play. There was nothing that could stop me from realizing my dream because from that point on, I was hooked.

It was hard at first though, I didn't have talent to get into music schools or money for private guitar teachers, nor musical experience, so I had to learn all by myself. All I had was a cheap acoustic guitar, internet and a strong will. Luckily, with all my desire to learn, it was more than enough. First I learned all the basic chords and how to read tabs. After a few weeks I was able to hold and switch between most of the basic open chords and play some simple songs. At that point I simply couldn't stop playing.

Or so I thought... Soon after, the inspiration suddenly ran out, and I reached my very first plateau. I became frustrated, I lost the desire to learn and inspiration to play. It felt like I hit a brick wall and couldn't progress any further. I didn't understand this at first, but I decided that I should stick with guitar anyway. I managed to get back on track with some inspiration that came out of nowhere. Later I found out that reaching plateaus like that is perfectly normal, it's something that happens to everyone; and just like that, I was back on track.

As my guitar journey went on, times like that - when I completely doubted my ability and questioned if I'm capable enough for this, got more often. I would then give in to the negative thoughts in my head like: you don't have any talent, you're tone deaf, you can't sing, this guitar sounds bad... Looking back I realize it was ridiculous and it hindered my progress a lot.

If you ever find yourself in a similar situation please remember: it's only the thoughts in your head, and the thoughts got you started in the first place. Negative thoughts will always come and go. Do not allow them to control your life! If you lose inspiration, you will lose interest, and that leads to quitting. At that times you just need to find some inspiration again, go back to your core values and reflect upon your goals! The inspiration will come back, but only if you stick with it, trust me.

A few years later, I was in a band. I fulfilled my dream of playing a real gig! It was an awesome experience even though I still felt like an amateur. At the same time I got the chance to help some people learn how to play guitar and I really liked it.

All that helped me become better as a guitar player, simply because I was playing with other people, and at the same time I gained more confidence in my playing. That transferred into other aspects of my life as well. Playing guitar helped me grow as a person and it can do the same for you.

You can start to learn guitar for whatever reason you choose. The problem is that people usually tend to give up after reaching their first plateaus because they lack the strong enough desire, they might find it too hard to even bother, or they make up excuses like "I don't have enough time to practice". You need to ask yourself: How badly do I want to play guitar? I talk more about the importance of the mindset later in the book.

Music is all about sharing and that's exactly why I wrote this book. I wanted to share with you the things that I've learned along the way, that will help you become a great guitar player! I'm not a professional guitar teacher, but I know that I can help you get this immensely valuable skill under your belt, fast! I also hope that I'm able to inspire you to learn guitar and minimize the frustrations and negative feelings that go along with learning any new skill. It is my way of giving back on everything that learning this instrument did for me.

This book was written by a guitar player for a guitar player.

Even if you can spare only 5 minutes each day to practice, you can learn how to play. There should be no excuses!

Chapter 1 - Guitars 101 and the Mindset

In this chapter you'll find everything that you should know about guitars in general, how they work, what are the most common types you can buy, what styles they're good for, what accessories do you need, etc. You'll find out how to choose the best guitar for beginners - a very important topic for people who haven't bought their first guitar yet.

If you already bought your first guitar you might wonder if it was the best choice, but don't worry. You can learn and practice on any guitar. What matters is that you like it and that it is properly set-up - meaning that the neck is straight, action fairly low, it doesn't go out of tune easily, intonation is correct, etc. More on all that later.

I'll also talk about the mindset and why too many people give up on guitar, and how to not be one of them.

Most common guitar types

Understanding the common guitar types and how they work (produce sound) is very important and beneficial to your knowledge as a guitar player. That's why I'm going to explain the four most popular types of guitars that you're going to encounter in music shops and online. They all have some major differences between them which determine their use. The four main types we'll talk about are: electric, acoustic, classical and bass guitars.

1. Electric guitars and amps

Electric guitar uses a pickup which contains magnets to catch the vibrations of metal guitar strings when you play. The pickup translates those vibrations into electrical impulses and then they are sent through the guitar cable to an amp. These electrical impulses are weak and that's why they need to be amplified with an amp before going through the speaker (which is often part of an amp).

The signal that electric guitar produces can be easily altered with the amps settings and effects, and an effect pedal, to add 'color' to the sound. That's why you can produce a wide range of different sounds (tones) on an electric guitar, from clean to distorted, and with different effects such as: reverb, chorus, delay etc.

There are two major guitar companies that contributed the most to electric guitars being what they are today. Those are Fender and Gibson. You can recognize them instantly by their body shape. Almost all other brands that appeared after are hugely influenced and inspired by one of these two families.

Electric guitars are the most versatile type of guitars used for all kinds of musical genres, ranging from jazz to metal. They are easier to play and feel softer when played because their strings are generally thinner than the strings on other guitars, and their neck is also narrower. Therefore, holding the chords and playing solos is the easiest on an electric guitar.

What about the amps?

You can practice and play on an electric guitar without an amp, but if you really want to unleash all its power and enjoy the full benefits, you'll need a nice quality amp, if you can afford it. There are two main types of electric guitar amps: solid state amps and valve or tube amps.

Solid state or digital amps are usually a good choice for beginners (which is debatable since there are some good ones, and often 'not good at all' ones) because they are less delicate and require less maintenance. They use solid state electronics like transistors to amplify the guitar signal. These amps are a lot cheaper and some of them have become really good nowadays even at a budget price.

A tube amp simply put uses at least one vacuum tube to amplify a guitar signal. They are based on an old - outdated technology, but that does not mean that the sound quality is 'outdated' too. As a matter of fact, many guitar players prefer their natural sound, especially distortion, and think they have have a much better sound quality over the newer digitalized technologies. These amps are also more expensive and harder to maintain. They are considered to produce better quality sound and are used extensively by professionals and players of all skill levels all over the world.

The thing is, as I've said, solid state amps have become really good and very reliable, and sometimes the difference in tone and sound quality is not even noticeable enough to justify the big difference in price.

Another thing to note is that many amps today are not just all tube or solid state only, but the mixes of both. These are called "hybrid amps". They use the best of both worlds - tubes for shaping the tone, and solid state transistors for their power section (making them more reliable). They feel closer to tube amps in tonal warmth, but the fact is that many professional guitar players play mostly on full tube/valve amps and always prefer their sound over any other amp type.

It's important to know that an amp will have the <u>biggest</u> impact on your sound, more than a guitar itself! So my advice is to always buy the best amp that you can, but only after trying it in a music shop. Avoid the really cheap ones and go for valves if you can.

2. Acoustic steel string guitars

Unlike electric guitars, acoustic guitars have hollow body which acts as a resonant box. It naturally (acoustically) strengthens and enhances the vibrations of guitar strings. If you play an acoustic guitar in a closed room, or in a tunnel for example (like a lot of the street guitar players, a.k.a. buskers do), those vibrations would be even more 'amplified', and you would hear a beautiful, deep and resonant sound.

That's the power of the acoustics. One big advantage over the electrics is that you can easily carry them around and play them anywhere since they don't require the use of an amp. The downside is that they are generally harder to play, their neck is wider and their steel strings are thicker and harder to press down on a guitar neck.

While the playability and versatility of an acoustic guitar is lower than on an electric, the acoustics have their own unique sound and charm. They are used in almost every musical genre. Even though they're not as versatile as electric guitars, you can play on them anything that you want really; but they're most suitable for rhythm playing (strumming), blues, pop, rock, country, fingerstyle and hybrid style song arrangements, etc.

Some guitar players would naturally prefer acoustics, others electrics, but you can't really compare the two because they are quite different. If you're not sure the best is to start on one and at some point try the other, with time you'll find out which type appeals to you the most.

Understanding the acoustic guitar sub-types

Acoustic guitar is a wider term for all guitars that produce sound acoustically. While its hard to classify them, there are certain sub-types that you need to know about and I'll do my best to explain them.

What I talked about so far applied only to acoustic **steel string** guitars, which are by far the most popular and widely known sub-type, and therefore referred to only as the 'acoustic guitars'.

There are many other sub-types of an acoustic guitar depending on their body type, size, material of the strings, the way in which they're played; then there are music genre specific acoustic guitars like flamenco guitars, slide guitars, etc. I'll just briefly explain the ones that you should know about for now so that you don't get confused.

Electro-acoustic guitars or acoustic electrics are like standard hollow body acoustic guitars but with electronics (a pickup) fitted into them so that they can be amplified with an acoustic amp or a PA system. These guitars are usually meant to be played live and are more expensive. They should sound good and be loud enough even when they are played unplugged (without electronics).

Semi-acoustic guitars on the other hand are usually electric guitars but with a semi-hollow (semi-acoustic) body. They have pickups like electric guitar and feel more like an electric guitar when you play them. They are very heavy and they need an amp to be loud enough. They combine the electric and the acoustic sound which is quite a unique combination. These are often used by jazz players.

Other notable sub-types of an acoustic guitar are: twelve-string, banjo, lap-steel, two-neck guitars, ukulele, harp guitar, baritone guitar, parlor guitar, acoustic bass guitar, guitarlele...

3. Acoustic nylon string guitars

These guitars are also very common and widely used, but many people who are new to guitar at first don't recognize the physical difference between these and acoustic steel strings.

The one major difference is that they are (obviously) fitted with nylon strings, which greatly affects their tone and playability. They also have even wider necks and smaller bodies. They're easier to play because nylon strings are much softer than the steel strings, but at the same time they are harder to play because of the wider necks.

The wider neck implies that they are supposed to be played in a classical playing position. In any case, you can get used to the neck even if you play in a regular playing position, which I'll explain later.

Classical nylon string guitars are most widely known for their use in music schools and for classical music genre. There are many other genre specific sub-types of classical guitars, such as: Gypsy guitars, Russian guitars, Flamenco guitars, Baroque guitars, Romantic guitars, etc. and they all have unique shapes and sounds.

Classical nylon string guitars (or simply - classical guitars) along with the acoustic steel string guitars (acoustic guitars) are the most common types of guitars that people usually buy.

4. Bass guitars

Although very different from the ones we've talked about so far, bass guitars still fit in a 'guitar' category. Bass guitars are a world of their own and they have a special place in all music. Bass is like a magical force that ties everything together in a song or a band. It's hard to imagine a band without a bass guitar player.

Basses can be played much like standard guitars, you can play lead (solos) with them, but they usually play a supportive role in a band along with the drums, while guitars are more out front in the spotlight. Bass guitar players must really know their stuff because they carry a lot of responsibility for the groove and rhythm feel in a band, and those are the most important for sounding good.

Basses are quite different than standard guitars. They produce a deep, low and vibrant sound. They have larger bodies, longer necks, and only 4 metal strings that are much thicker than the strings on a standard guitar - making their tuning one octave lower.

They are usually played with fingers by plucking or slapping the strings, but they can be played with a pick too. There is a variety of different techniques and styles for playing a bass guitar that are used for all kinds of music genres, the choice of which depends on your preferences.

There are electric bass guitars and acoustic bass guitars. Electric basses require an amp made specifically for basses (they are not loud enough without an amp even if it's for practice only), while the acoustic basses can be played on their own.

One of the absolute best combinations to hear live is an acoustic guitar combined with an acoustic bass guitar. Acoustic basses can be quite costly, while the electric bases you can buy for a more reasonable price.

One of the funniest questions I've seen someone ask is: "If I suck at guitar, should I pick up bass instead?" :)

To answer seriously to this question, if you think that you suck on guitar and want to quit, then you'll suck on the bass as well. Each instrument requires your hard work and dedication. You can learn to play **any** instrument but what matters the most is that you choose the one(s) that you want to play.

How to choose the best first guitar (The right way)

If you don't have any previous experience with buying guitars it can be really difficult to choose the best one. Most people don't know what to look for in a guitar, what guitar will best suit their needs and how to try out guitars in a music shop.

The best place to start is to ask yourself:

- What kind of music do I like to play?

- What type of guitar do I prefer?

- How much money am I willing to spend?

- What are my goals with playing guitar?

- Do I want to be able to play only for me and my friends, strum a few chords at parties, or more?

The thing is, I can't tell you what guitar is best for you because I don't know what your goals and your wishes are. If you are not sure what those are, you can discover them if you ask yourself those questions and look for the answers within.

I can only give you certain guidelines and a couple of recommendations based on my experience. The key word here is experience. Only through gaining experience by playing different guitars, styles, genres, etc. will you be able to know what you like best. What matters most is that you start and learn the basics, and everything else will fall in its place. So don't worry too much about finding that perfect guitar.

In the previous section I've explained the most common types of guitars that you can buy, and hopefully you have an idea about the different options to consider. You have to keep in mind a few things when buying your first guitar:

1. You can play any kind of music on any guitar. It's just that some types are more suitable for certain styles than others. If your wish is to play death metal, then a pink classical guitar probably isn't the wisest choice. The genre of music that you see yourself playing the most in the near future should determine what kind of guitar you buy.

2. Your first guitar won't be your last. After a certain time of practicing, playing and getting better on guitar, you'll most likely want to expand and buy another guitar, usually of different type. Then after some time again you'll want to buy another, and then another, and soon you might find out that you suffer from widely known 'Guitar Acquisition Syndrome (GAS)'. This is serious. :) I've been playing for almost ten years and right now I have four guitars, and I'm still thinking about buying new ones. It's a normal process of you growing as a guitar player, but hard on the budget for most people.

3. Electric guitar is the most versatile type of guitar. With an electric guitar you can manipulate the sound in almost unlimited number of ways. You can even make it sound like an acoustic with the use of an amp, effect pedals, pickups, etc. (although it can never be 100% the same sound and feel). It's also somewhat easier to start with. If you like to play any kind of metal with a lot of distortion, hard rock, punk, buy an electric. If your goal is to play in a band soon, it's better to buy an electric. If you would like to be a lead guitar player and play captivating solos, buy an electric. If you feel that you incline more toward the electric, buy an electric. Simple as that. :)

4. It's best to avoid really cheap guitars. Let's face it, playing music is a quite expensive hobby for most people. That's why you have to know what you pay for.

Many cheap guitars usually come at a price - they seem really good at the beginning but later you may find out that they are horrible sounding compared to other guitars, hard to play, break more easily, go out of tune while playing and cause tons of other problems.

Even though there are a couple of gems out there which are quality made at low price, it's best to avoid them altogether if you can, and save money and invest a little bit more at the beginning. I know that's hard but it will pay of in the end and you'll be more satisfied.

The problem with cheap guitars is that they are mass produced in large factories (usually in some Asian countries) by guitar companies which want to satisfy the growing demands of the market as fast as possible, and get profit. Little care is given to the quality of their build because there is not much human element involved, and that's why out of every 10 guitars there's bound to be a couple that come with serious problems that get overlooked. If you're like me, you'll want a nice instrument for yourself which is reliable and will last.

You don't have to spend a fortune on your first guitar, just make sure that it's a quality instrument. Soon I'll share with you how to do that.

5. If you're left-handed, you need to buy a left-handed guitar. It will save you a lot of trouble at the beginning. It's always better to do what feels most natural. There is no point in forcing yourself otherwise when there are plenty of options available for left-handed guitar players. Not as much, yes, but enough.

With that being said, you can learn to play on a right-handed guitar even if you are left-handed, if there are no other options. I have a friend who learned to play that way and he hasn't had any problems. Jimi Hendrix (the most famous electric guitar player) was left-handed but he played right-handed guitars with their strings flipped over. He taught himself to be both-handed. He could play just about anything on guitar.

6. Always try a guitar before buying it. No matter what anyone else says and suggests you to buy, you need to see and feel that guitar with your own hands. Even if you can't play anything at least hold a couple of guitars in your lap and hands and see which one feels best.

- Here's a guide for beginners on how to try out guitars in a music shop

1) Find a music store. If you know someone who is experienced with guitars ask them to accompany you. While you're there, browse around the store and see if you like something. Ask people who work there to give you some suggestions and explain that you're a beginner. They will most likely ask you about your budget first.

   Be careful if you tell them that you're looking for your first guitar. They might suggest you one of those 'starter packs' that are horrible quality and should be avoided. You can also research their site on the internet and have a list of guitars that you would like to try out.

2) Choose a guitar that you like and ask the person you've brought along if he/she can play something. If you don't know someone who plays a guitar, or they couldn't come with you, ask anyone who works there if they can demonstrate the guitar for you.

   Listen closely to how the guitar sounds like when they play. Notice if you can hear any noticeable bad sounding fret buzz or ringing type of noise; if there is any, the guitar will probably need a setup later, which is an extra cost.

3) Now try holding the guitar in your hands and get the feel for it. Try to play each string and strum it a bit. Play some notes by pressing the strings on a guitar neck between the frets. Feel free to ask the personnel to help you with this as well.

   Try not to be self-conscious and shy like many of us are at the music stores. :) The job of the people who work their is to help you however they can, and they will be happy to do so. Also, don't worry about how you play or how bad you might sound. Just remember that we've all been there, nobody will laugh or judge you, and you shouldn't judge yourself.

4) When you are done, choose another guitar. Notice the difference. Try at least a couple of guitars and compare them. Which one felt the best and you liked the most?

Only buy a guitar that **you** liked the best, but at the same time be open-minded and consider the advice or recommendation(s) that someone with more experience is giving you.

But if you notice that someone is intentionally trying to persuade you into buying something, don't listen to them. Music stores usually offer so called 'starter packs' for beginners, for a very low price, in which you get: a guitar, a gig bag, picks and a couple of other nifty tools. These starter packs have often proved to be really bad quality, they're not worth your money and your time.

When you go to a music shop you have to act in a way that you'll only settle for the best quality guitar for your money, and you'll buy only what you personally like and feel like buying.

Electric guitar recommendations

If you're not sure what type of guitar to buy, it's safer to go with an electric as they are more versatile instruments. They are also easier to start with because their strings are thinner and their necks are narrower, which makes the learning process easier.

There are some really great quality electric guitars at a low price like: Yamaha Pacifica, Fender Mexican Stratocaster, Epiphone, Ibanez... I recommend you to also check out a guitar called Chapman ML-1 by Chapman guitars. It's a guitar company and brand created by Rob Chapman. He's an artist, guitar player and a guitar guru. He has a very popular and helpful channel on Youtube.

His guitars are the best value for money I've seen so far, and Rob Chapman is a great guy and great guitar player as well. By the way, this is my honest opinion and I'm not sponsored by Chapman guitars in any way.

Acoustic guitar recommendations

As for the acoustics, you can start on them too and that won't be mistake. I have started on the acoustic and I play acoustics primarily. Most players today are starting on the acoustics that are on the cheaper side in the budget category.

You have to be a little bit more careful when choosing a budget acoustic guitar because of the problems I talked about. You can avoid all those if you go to a music shop and try them out in a way that I've described, and also if you research online and read about the experiences of other buyers of that guitar, how high is its rating, is it popular, is it recommended, etc.

You can also search on Youtube for video reviews and demonstrations of that guitar (if it's a popular guitar there will be many videos) and hear what it sounds like.

You always have to do a little bit of research first if you want to buy the best quality guitar for your money, especially if its the first one.

There are many different acoustic guitar body shapes and sizes that you can choose from. What you will most often see are shapes like dreadnought, jumbo, baby, parlor, classical shape, concert, grand concert... Different manufacturers often have unique shapes. Different body shapes are better for playing certain styles, but for a beginner this doesn't really matter. Just choose a shape that you like and which feels the most comfortable.

As for the size, most manufacturers use 4/4 style system to state the size of an acoustic guitar. You can buy a smaller sized guitar (3/4) if it's a travel guitar, if it's meant for a little kid, or it's just something that you prefer.

Don't worry if you think that you have small hands because your fingers adapt.

Some of the best acoustic guitars that I can recommend in a lower price range are: Takamine GD10, Jasmine S, Yamaha C40 (Classical), Seagull S6 (a little bit pricier than the others but amazing sounding), Epiphone PR-150, Yamaha FG700s.

Recommended mid-price range guitars are: Taylor 110e, Epiphone EJ-200CE, anything from Maton (mid to high end), Takamine EF341SC, Takamine Hirade series (high end classicals).

Necessary mindset - how to practice, reach your goals, and not give up

Probably the most important section in this book. Having the right mindset determines whether you achieve any sort of success or not. Your ideal mindset should be: "I will easily learn guitar no matter what obstacles come in my way!"

Before you start learning and practicing there are a few things you need to be aware of:

1. Learning guitar takes time and dedication.

2. Having talent is overrated and not necessary.

3. Only through dedicated and deliberate practice, and by enjoying and having fun, will you achieve your goals on guitar.

4. There is a difference between "practice" and "playing".

5. As with any other area of your life it's important to set goals, especially for learning guitar.

6. You will lose motivation and inspiration and you'll hit roadblocks sometimes but that's something we all have to deal with.

Now let's elaborate on this further.

Talent Vs Hard work

If you're thinking that you must be talented in order to enjoy and play music on guitar, think again. Anyone can learn to play a guitar no matter what there background is. 90% of success comes from hard work, it also comes from: imagination, inspiration, motivation, social support, environment, your cognitive abilities (which is something that can be developed), creativity, personality, luck...

It may be easier for some people to learn, someone can be more musical by nature, but it's just because they're more in touch with their inner musician. I'm a firm believer that we all have music inside of ourselves - the ability to be musical and create music. That's why it's not the matter of talent, it's just the matter of digging deep enough to free that inner musician and unlock the creativity that is within all of us. You cannot write the stories until you have learned the language!

Good days Vs Bad days

For anyone that has been playing guitar for some time it is a well known fact that there are "good guitar days" and there are "bad days".

Good days are the ones when you feel inspired, you learn new things easily, you feel progress, practice seems very enjoyable and everything seems to flow.

Bad days on the other hand are the ones when you feel a lack of inspiration and motivation to practice and play anything. Whatever you try to play doesn't sound good to you or you make mistakes you wouldn't have otherwise.

This is where a lot of new guitar players get confused and discouraged. They start to learn guitar full of motivation and passion and as soon as the bad days come, they feel like all they learned was for nothing since they didn't see the results they expected.

They start sabotaging themselves by saying:

- guitar is too hard to learn,

- I'm not talented enough,

- I'm too old to start now,

- I have small hands,

- I don't have enough time,

- I lack motivation... Name any excuse.

That opens the doors to quitting. The truth is that these bad days when you don't feel like picking up a guitar and playing are perfectly normal and happen to everyone from time to time!

What matters the most is that you acknowledge these feelings and thoughts when they happen and understand that they are just feelings and thoughts that come and go, and they will always come and go, but they're not the actual facts.

The actual fact is that you're a someone who is taking action towards realizing his dream of playing guitar. Anyone who is dedicated and takes action regardless of the drawbacks and obstacles is going to be successful. That's the law of attraction of life.

There is a great quote I once heard: "In life you don't attract what you want, you attract what you are. " If you are constantly taking action and you're practicing, then you <u>are</u> a guitar player my friend.

Practice and Playing

You'll notice that throughout this book I'm constantly differentiating the terms 'play' and 'practice'. There is a difference between "playing" and "practicing". When you're practicing your mind should be focused on your practice and nothing else. You should not let your mind drift too much. You also need to make conscious effort to avoid making any mistakes, because mistakes slow down your progress and can lead to developing bad habits in your technique.

You avoid the mistakes by always practicing **slowly** at first and then gradually speeding up. Practicing deliberately and slowly first, and focusing the attention to what you're doing, makes you practice more efficiently and you experience progress much faster. Of course, we're all humans and not robots, we tend to lose concentration, make mistakes, procrastinate or doubt ourselves. We just have to deal with all that, there is no way around it, and sometimes it's not an easy thing to do.

Practice is important because it leads to developing **muscle memory**. Muscle memory allows you to play freely, without thinking too much about where your hands and fingers should go. This allows you clear the way in your head for all the emotions to come out in your playing.

It may sound poetic, but that's how it really is. You can only play something (a chord or a song for example) after you've practiced it so much that you don't have to think about it anymore at all, and you can play it in your sleep. Repetition in your practice is key for developing this ability.

You'll experience this after you learn your first chord. Your fingers will just form the chord shape almost instantly and you won't have to think about how to correctly grip it anymore.

We practice so that we can play freely, have fun and fully experience the music that we're playing. Not thinking about technique helps with that. You should reserve some time each day just for playing guitar, be it anything that you know, and enjoy. That's what keeps you going. It's important to not get stuck in a practicing mode only.

Setting goals

For you as an individual and a guitar player it's important to have a clear long-term goal in sight, which is divided into smaller goals, and a sense of progression - when you notice you are moving toward your goal and getting better as time passes. Maybe you want to play live gigs, or you want to write your own songs, or just jam with your buddies on an acoustic guitar for fun, or all that... Whatever it is, once you have your long-term goal of what you want to achieve in one, two, three, five years or more, always remember it, and imagine as if you've already achieved it, especially when you need motivation. Feel free to dream!

By using this visualization technique you will make sure that you stay on track and not lose the end goal in sight.

You also need to have a sense of your mid-term and short-term goals which are bringing you closer toward your greater, long-term goal. These can be anything, for example: doing some specific technique exercises (like chord changes), learning about music theory for better improvising and songwriting, training your ear in a musical way to become a better musician, reading a guitar learning book (like this one) or watching helpful videos online...

I've said many times, but the most important thing for any guitarist is to build a strong foundation. One of your goals at the beginning should be to get all the basics down from which you can build upon later and develop further into any direction that you want.

The best way to achieve that fast is if you know "what" and "how" to practice right from the start and every step of the way. You can get that with a good guitar teacher, by using a book or simply by using the internet. Though it is hard to find all this information structured in a right way online without paying for some expensive $100 DVDs, guitar teachers (it's hard to find the ones that are right) or membership sites. That's why with this book, you are in a right place. ;)

Remember that it doesn't matter how good you are on guitar and what your skill level is. Playing music shouldn't be thought of as a competition at who's better than whom. Only thing that matters is how much you enjoy playing music and sharing it with others. There's no point in comparing yourself to other guitar players.

Just take it slow, be patient and enjoy everything as much as you can, and everything will come to it's place. I promise.

Guitar parts explained

- There are 3 main parts of any guitar:

1. Guitar body (top, back and sides),

2. Guitar neck

3. Guitar headstock

1. Body of an acoustic guitar

Guitar body is the largest guitar part. It's made out of selected types of woods and it acts as a resonant box. Therefore it has the biggest impact on the color of the sound that a guitar produces. While the acoustic guitar body is hollow, the electric guitar body is solid and heavier.

On an acoustic body you'll find: guitar bridge, a soundhole, a pickguard (not always) and strap buttons.

Guitar bridge is also made of wood and is found behind the soundhole, where the strings begin. It's purpose is to hold the strings in place with the string pegs. The string pegs are usually white color and made from plastic. They need to be pressed in firmly in the bridge to prevent the strings from popping out. Electric guitars don't have string pegs but different mechanisms to hold the strings in place.

Soundhole of an acoustic guitar allows it to better absorb the vibrations of guitar strings. The sound which is created by those vibrations enters the soundhole, bounces around, and then comes back out stronger and better. You can feel that the whole body of a guitar shakes and vibrates while playing.

Pickguard or a scratch plate, as the name suggests, protects the body of a guitar from scratching or hitting with a pick while playing. Some guitars have them, some don't. Some guitar brands like Taylor guitars have uniquely shaped pickguards.

Strap buttons are found on the bottom of a guitar and on the back in the upper body region toward the headstock. They allow you to hook the guitar to a strap and play it while standing up. Usually they are not enough for your guitar to be safe from falling on the ground accidentally so in addition to guitar straps, strap locks are often used by guitarists.

2. Guitar neck

Guitar neck is what goes between the body of a guitar and a guitar headstock. It's usually made out of two types of wood: one for the neck itself, and one for the fingerboard which goes on top of it (it's where we place our fingers to play the notes). Guitar neck consists of: a guitar nut, frets or fretwires, fingerboard or fretboard, dot-inlays, and a truss rod.

Guitar nut is a piece of plastic with small slits that guitar strings go through. It connects a guitar neck with a headstock. It can be made from different materials such as: bone, metal, graphite. It needs to be strong enough to sustain the friction from the guitar strings. If it's not strong enough (not made from a good material) it will have negative effect on the tuning stability and can impact the guitar sound.

Fretwires are small pieces of metal that lay across the fretboard, and frets are just the spaces between the fretwires. However, it is very common for fretwires to be simply called "**frets**", so don't let that confuse you.

Fingerboard, also called a fretboard, is a piece of wood (types of woods most often used are: maple, rosewood and ebony) glued on top of a guitar neck. It's a place where you have to press down the strings with your fingers, between the frets, in order to play different notes. This is where you'll spend most of your time studying on a guitar.

Dot-Inlays are there to help you navigate the fretboard as you play. Sometimes they are not included (on classical guitars for example). They are used as a point of reference or position markers, to help you quickly figure out where you are, and what scale, solo or a chord you're playing.

Truss rod is a steel rod or a steel bar which runs inside the neck along it's length. It is used to adjust the tension of a guitar neck, or in other words, to provide relief or increase tension that the strings are making by increasing or decreasing the curvature of a guitar neck (lengthwise). It is adjusted with an allen key. By straightening the neck - tension increases, and similarly if the neck is loosened, tension decreases.

Adjustment of the truss rod has an effect on a guitar '**action**'. The action is simply a distance between the strings and a guitar fingerboard. If the action is low, guitar will be easier to play, but you might hear a note/fret buzz-like sound on some notes, because the action is not set up properly. If the action is too high, there might not be any fret buzz but it will be too difficult to play. Some players prefer the action which is a little bit on the higher side in order to "fight" the note a bit, while others like their action to be low and even. But Keep in mind that height of a guitar bridge is the main contributing factor to guitar action.

In the end, it all comes down to your personal preference, but a good setup is always the key to having a guitar which is very playable. If you're new to guitar this should be done by an expert, and also you should ask for low action because it will be easier to learn and play with less difficulties.

3. Guitar headstock

This is a part where you can tune your guitar. When guitar is in tune it will sound the best. You should learn to hear and check if your guitar is in tune, although this will come naturally in time with experience. On the headstock you can find: a tuning mechanism with tuners which you can turn clockwise and counter-clockwise to change the pitch of the strings. There is also a logo of a guitar company and sometimes a serial number. Some guitars have reverse headstocks (pointed upwards), some have more symmetrical headstocks, and some have standard headstocks pointed downwards.

Electric guitar specific parts

Those include: pickups, volume and tone knobs, pickup selector, input jack socket... Sometimes there are more parts, but these are the main ones.

Pickups of an electric guitar are found on a guitar body, between the bridge and the neck, under the guitar strings. They contain magnets - one for each string, which "pick-up" the string vibrations and transfer them into electrical impulses.

There are two most common types of pickups: single-coils and humbuckers. Humbuckers have 'fatter' sound and they are often used for playing heavier music. They are always found on Gibson guitars. Single coils are almost always found on Fender guitars. The choice of which type to use comes down to your personal preferences.

A pickup which is closer to the neck is called the "neck pickup", and the one closer to the bridge - "bridge" pickup. On most Fender and other Fender-like guitars there is also a pickup in the middle - "middle pickup". All these different positions of the pickups give a little bit different sound. You can hear this for yourself if you use an acoustic guitar or an unplugged electric guitar. Pluck the strings near the bridge and then pluck them near the neck, and you will hear the difference.

When a string is plucked it vibrates with larger amplitude at the neck, and with less amplitude at the bridge. You'll notice that as you move closer to the bridge the sound becomes thinner and brighter. Closer to the neck the sound becomes louder, deeper, darker and more vibrant. This is the exact reason why we usually have more than one pickup on an guitar. Bridge pickups are designed to be higher output than the neck pickups in order to compensate for the thinner sound. That's why they are often used for solos and more aggressive playing. The choice of which pickup position to use again depends solely on a guitar players preference.

Pickup selector as the name suggests lets you select which pickup is being used at the particular moment. Standard Fender guitars have 3 pickups and a five-way selector switch that lets you choose individual pickups or different combinations of the pickups. Guitars with 2 pickups have a three-way selector switch that lets you choose between the neck pickup, bridge pickup or both.

Volume knob is simply a knob which you can turn and change the volume of your electric guitar signal. If your guitar has two or more pickups it might also have more than one volume knob for each pickup.

Tone knob cuts out the high frequencies of the strings to a certain degree. It's hard to explain exactly what it does, you have to turn it around and hear for yourself. Most guitar players just keep the tone knob at 10 (maximum level) and use the amp settings to adjust these controls (bridge, middle and treble).

Input jack socket is a socket where you can plug your guitar with a guitar cable, which on the other end goes to the amplifier.

Essential guitar accessories

Practicing and playing guitar often requires the use of certain tools which make your life easier and help you become a better guitar player faster. You're going to need them sooner or later so in this section you'll get to know what those tools are and why are they useful.

Guitar tuner is a device which helps you get your guitar in tune. Being in tune means that all guitar strings vibrate exactly at certain frequencies. If you just started playing guitar, having a guitar tuner will help you immensely. The simple reason for that is that you sound better when you are in tune.

Guitars sometimes go out of tune even if you didn't do anything to cause that, which is perfectly normal. There are many outside factors that can cause tuning instability problems, like humidity or temperature change.

If you're a beginner you probably haven't gotten used to hearing when a guitar is exactly in tune. A tuner helps you remember that "in tune" guitar sound which is why it's so important to use it right from the start and tune your guitar regularly. With time, you'll be able to tune a guitar by ear, but you'll still use a tuner from time to time to get in tune quickly.

In the old days people used things like pitch pipes and tuning forks, but today electronic tuners are used almost exclusively. Electronic tuner shows you which note is heard (through the microphone) when you play it on guitar. It usually has a display and LED indicators which show you whether you need to tune a guitar string up or down and change its pitch. They require the use of one or two standard alkaline batteries to operate. These tuners can be especially useful if you're playing a gig and you need to tune your guitar quickly in a loud environment. Some acoustic guitars come with this kind of tuners built into their bodies. These are usually instruments aimed for beginner guitar players.

There are also so called "clip on" tuners which can be attached to different instruments. Clip on tuners are usually able to eliminate the background noise because they have a vibration sensor instead of the microphone which is found on the standard tuners.

Another type of electronic tuners that are widely used are in the form of Android/iOS apps. What's really good about them is that they:

- Help you tune your guitar

- Are usually free

I have a couple of tuners but I find myself most often using just an app. The app that I use and recommend is called DaTuner Lite. It's free app and it does its job really well.

Finally, the strobe tuners. These are the most accurate type of tuners, you can read all about how they work on Wikipedia. Problem with them is that they are really expensive so I don't recommend buying these if you are just starting out. Regular tuner will serve you just fine in the beginning.

Guitar strap is simply a strap which you can attach to the strap buttons on guitar, and it allows you to play while standing up. It can be made from different materials, but it's very important that is comfortable and that it doesn't put a strain on your shoulder.

Many guitar players have hard time with choosing the optimal strap height and playing while standing up. Most prefer their guitars to hang low, near the waist line (take a look at Slash as an extreme example), others like them to be at the same height as when they're in a sitting position. It's a matter of personal preference, just keep in mind that if you're used to playing your guitar in a sitting position, playing guitar while standing up will take some time to get used to, so don't get discouraged if it's really awkward at first.

Another thing to keep in mind is that a guitar can fall down especially if you really get 'crazy' while playing, so most players use strap locks to make sure that their guitar doesn't fall down. Some guitar straps (more expensive ones) come with special attaching mechanisms that lock the strap to a strap button thus making it impossible to accidentally fall down. You can also buy separate strap locks which save your guitar from falling and breaking, and they shouldn't be expensive.

Guitar picks are made from different materials ranging from plastic to metal. They are usually shaped like a triangle with oval edges, and come in various thicknesses, shapes and sizes.

Most beginners usually start to strum guitar with their fingers because it's easier and feels more natural. Playing and strumming with a pick however requires some time to get used to it, but it will become second nature soon if you stick with it.

To make this process of getting used to playing with a pick faster, you'll want to buy a thinner pick at the beginning (the one that bends a little when applying pressure - up to 1 millimeters). It's best to buy a couple because it's really easy for them to get lost. Then you can move on to the thicker picks (above 1 mm). Thicker picks (when you get used to playing with them) can give your more response and control while playing faster, as well as louder, sharper and brighter sound.

The choice of the best guitar pick: shape, material, size and thickness, in the end comes down to personal preference. It takes a lot of experimenting to find the perfect one of you. In that regard, it's best to try as many different picks as possible over time, and after a few years of playing you'll know which guitar picks are the best choice for your playing style.

Metronome is something that every musician should have and use. It's a device that produces a simple "click" on the beat sound at a steady tempo that you choose. It's one of the most well known practice tools for learning to feel the beat and keep the time while playing. It is therefore an essential practice tool for any musician.

Can you guess what is the most important skill for playing guitar or any other instrument, and sounding good? It is the ability to feel where the beat is and keep time, and the ability to 'play with the beats'. If you can do that you'll sound like a pro even if you play with just two chords. If you play in front of an audience and do your job right, people will notice even subconsciously and start moving and clapping their hands with the beat of the music that you are playing. That's one of the key elements to sounding so good on any musical instrument that gets overlooked often.

The unit for tempo is BPM - Beats Per Minute. You can set the metronome to for e.g. 80 bpm, which means that it will produce 80 beats per minute, and it will keep going until you stop it or unless it runs out of batteries. More on metronome practice and why you should use it is in the strumming chapter.

There are mechanical and electrical metronomes. If you are new to guitar it's best just to buy an electric metronome, but don't go below $15. These metronomes are reliable, well made and durable, and they have many more added functions which are useful for rhythm practice.

There are also non-physical electric metronomes, either on the internet, or in the from of an app for Android/iOS. As far as the apps go I would stay away from the free ones unless they come from reputable developers, and have a good rating with many downloads. The reason is that it has often been shown that some of them are not accurate enough.

Guitar capo is a very useful tool in your guitar playing arsenal. While you may not find much use for it at the beginning, chances are you'll rely on it a lot later in your playing. What it does is it basically presses down all 6 strings across a guitar fret, thereby replacing the nut of a guitar. You can place it on any fret on the guitar neck. Why is this useful?

For starters, by using a guitar capo you can change keys easily. If you play a C, F and G chords in an open position (near the nut), you are playing in the key of C. If you take a capo and put it on the 2nd fret and play the same chords with the same shapes, you would actually be playing D, G and A chords in the key of D. The main thing is that you didn't have to change the chord shapes but you still changed the key, just by moving a capo. Don't worry if this doesn't make sense to you now. It will all become clear later.

Capos are made by various manufacturers, like: Kyser, Dunlop, G7th... They differ in their shape and construction. My advice is not to spend less than $10 on a capo because the ones that are really cheap won't do their job correctly - the strings would often go out of tune, and some strings would not ring out correctly.

There are also some special capos with special uses like: rolling capos (you can move the capo by rolling it <u>while</u> playing), or partial capos (they cover only a few strings that you choose, leaving the rest open). Players who use these capos really know what they're doing.

Sound recorder - First time I learned about the benefits of recording myself was from Tommy Emmanuel). In one of his live sessions he spoke about why is it so important to regularly record yourself while playing. The main benefit is that you can hear yourself how you actually sound like.

Listening to how you sound like on a recording is like hearing your playing from a listeners perspective. You will definitely notice some or many mistakes, that you wouldn't have noticed otherwise. You will hear and recognize the aspects of your playing that you don't like and need to improve. This is immensely useful for sounding good on guitar really fast!

This was a revelation for me back when I first started recording some of my own playing. I felt really confident and thought that my playing was great by my own standards, but when I heard the recordings of myself I had to face with the fact that even though I played all the notes correctly, I sounded bad because my rhythm and my timing were way off.

I also noticed that I sounded emotionless because I didn't incorporate the **dynamics** - that's when you increase or decrease the intensity of what you're playing depending on how you're feeling the song at the particular moment. Those things really make a big difference!

After realizing what I had to work on thanks to recording myself, I drastically improved my playing over the next few months. Then from time to time I would listen to the recordings made at the beginning and compared them to my new recordings. The change was more then evident. I was proud on myself because of all the progress that could be heard even from a listeners perspective.

I hope that you can see by now why using a sound recorder for your playing and practice right from the start is so much useful.

There are many options available for sound recording which I won't go into now. For beginners, a standard sound recorder will be quite enough for practice and keeping track of your progress. You should be able to find them at your local music shops.

Of course, there are also apps for your smartphone which help you record yourself, most of them are free. I actually use an app like this on my Android device. It does its job quite well and I'm very happy with it. It's called **Smart Voice Recorder**. I can honestly recommend that you try it, it's free, and the recorded sound quality is very good.

Jam buddy, although not necessarily an accessory, having one or more jam buddies with whom you can play guitar with is really beneficial, and it's one of the most fun and enjoyable things to do. If you don't know anyone else who is a musician, you should find someone to play/jam with. You can get to know new interesting people, form a band, play in parks with friends, communicate with each other through music... You can also practice together and motivate each other especially if you're on a similar skill level. You can offer guitar lessons to anyone whom you can teach something. This helps you as well by strengthening the knowledge that you already have.

I used to offer free guitar lessons to people with less experience than me, just so that I could find someone to jam with. I did that because I didn't know anyone else who played a guitar. I managed to help out a few people, and what I realized was that explaining something to someone else helped me as well to solidify what I already knew.

If you are lucky and you have (or you find) someone with much more experience than you, you can absorb from them, pick up their tricks, and learn much more quickly than if you were do it all by yourself.

You will progress much faster on guitar if you jam with other musicians, simple as that.

Gig-bag or a **guitar case** are needed to protect your guitar while traveling and carrying it around. If you want to travel with a guitar you'll most definitely want a quality guitar case because it's not rare that guitars get damaged in transport. Even that's not a guarantee, so people usually invest in a travel guitar - they are often smaller in size and more on the cheaper side.

Some guitars come with hard cases when you buy them, some with gig bags, but if you don't have any I would recommend that you buy one because you'll need something to carry your guitar in very soon.

Chapter 2 - Getting started

Ready to finally get started? In this section you're going to learn some music theory, the note circle, the names of the open strings on guitar, octave shapes, correct body posture and how to hold a guitar, how to play with a pick, how to read tabs and chord boxes, and much more!

Knowing this stuff is very important for any guitar player; it will get you ready in the best possible way for the next stage where you will learn the basic guitar chords and how to strum.

Understanding The Note circle

This is the most fundamental concept to know for anyone who wants play music on any instrument. I say this because everything that you learn later will correlate to this in some way. This is the foundation of all music that you hear today.

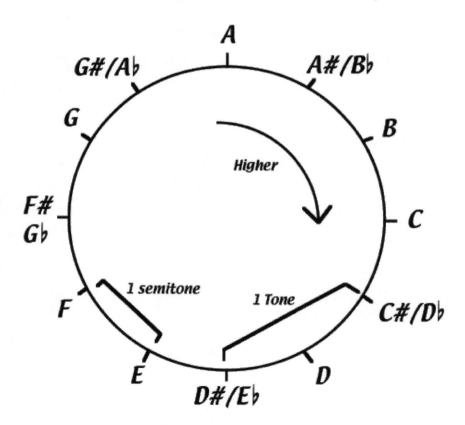

Image courtesy of justinguitar.com (awesome site, check it out!)

The note circle shows all 12 music notes that exist in Western music. Those notes are:

A ; A# or Bb ; B ; C ; C# or Db ; D ; D# or Eb ; E ; F ; F# or Gb ; G ; G# or Ab

It's important to remember this note order - which notes have sharps (#) or flats (b) between them, and which don't.

Notice that A# and Bb are exactly the same notes, and the same goes for C#/Db, D#/Eb, F#/Gb, G#/Ab. These 5 notes have different names but the same sound. The name which is being used (# - sharp or b - flat) depends on their purpose and their use in a particular situation in music theory.

Also note that there aren't any sharps or flats between notes B/C, and E/F. That's just how it is in Western music.

If you move clockwise around the circle, the notes become higher in pitch. If you move counter-clockwise the notes become lower in pitch.

The distance (in pitch) between any two notes is called an **interval**. All intervals have their names which we won't go into now as it is beyond the scope of this book. What's important for you to to know is that the distance between two notes that are next to each other (one step on the circle in any direction) is also called a **semitone**. Two semitones make one **tone**, which is two steps on the circle in any direction (as shown on picture).

How does this relate to a guitar?

Simple, one semitone is the smallest step on guitar - equal to one fret. If you take a guitar and play the note on the 5th fret of the thickest string (A note), and then you play the note on the 6th fret of the same string (A# or Bb note), that would be the step of one semitone, (which is often abbreviated to "S"). If instead of the 6th fret same string, you play the 7th fret (B note), that would be the step of one tone (often abbreviated to "T").

By moving up on the guitar fretboard (toward the bridge) in this way the notes are becoming higher in pitch, and by moving down the fretboard (toward the headstock) the notes are becoming lower in pitch.

The note on the 5th fret of the thickest string which I used for this example is an A note. When we played the note on the 6th fret of the same string, which is one semitone higher (clockwise on the circle), the note becomes A#, and one semitone lower (counter-clockwise on the circle) it becomes an Ab.

If we play the note on the 7th fret thickest string, which is one tone higher, the note would be B, and one tone lower, on the 3rd fret, the note would be G.

Guitar tuning and names of the open strings

You will often hear the term 'open' string(s) - it's just the term for one of the 6 guitar strings (or more) that are played without any fretted notes.

Guitar strings when played oscillate (vibrate) at certain frequencies thus producing different notes. In that regard, guitar strings by default are always tuned (by increasing or decreasing the tension with tuning pegs on the headstock) to vibrate at certain pre-determined frequencies.

That is called '**standard**' tuning, and from that tuning guitar strings get their names by the note they produce. The names are: E, A, D, G, B, e (thickest to thinnest string). All of the notes come from the note circle. Here is how it looks like on guitar:

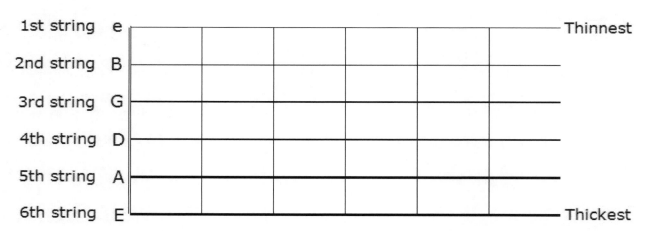

As an exercise you can try to workout how many steps there are between each of those notes with the help of the note circle. For example: E to A is 5 steps, meaning that there are 5 semitones, or 2 tones and 1 semitone, D to B is... You get the idea. You can do this for any of the notes from the note circle. This exercise helps you remember the note order which should be easy.

Notice that the thickest guitar string - E, and the thinnest - e, are the same notes. Note 'e' is just two <u>octaves</u> higher. I used the lower case letter 'e' for the thinnest string just so that you can distinguish them more easily.

There is a cool trick to remember string note names easily. The trick is to use the acronyms. For example:

- **E**ddie **A**te **D**ynamite **G**ood **B**ye **E**ddie; or

- **E**at **A**ll **D**ay **G**et **B**ig **E**asy.

You can make one for yourself if you want, the funnier you make it the easier you'll remember the names. :)

What is an octave?

An **octave** is the name for an interval which is the equivalent of going around the note circle once fully (which is 12 semitones) from the note that you start on, in this case E, and finishing on the same note but an octave higher (in pitch).

I've already said that guitar strings vibrate at certain frequencies (number of oscillations per unit of time) thus producing different notes. When one note is an octave higher than the other note (which is lower in pitch), it means that the string producing an octave higher note is vibrating exactly **2 times faster** than the lower one, and vice versa. Hopefully this makes sense.

How to find and remember any note anywhere on a guitar fretboard

Now you understand the note circle and the note order, how it applies to guitar, and you know the names of the open strings on guitar. You can use this knowledge to easily find any note anywhere on a guitar fretboard!

So how do you do this?

By using the note circle and by counting the steps, of course.

Let's start on an A string. The open A string is an A note which you can locate on the note circle. Next you look at the 1st fret of the A string on guitar. That note is one step up on the note circle, so it's A#. 2nd fret of the same string is B note, 3rd is C, 4th - C#, 5th - D... See how easy this is? Try to do this exercise for at least two more guitar strings, going all the way to the 12th fret.

6 key tones

There are faster ways to find the notes on guitar fingerboard. Next step would be to memorize the 6 key tones.

Those are the notes on the 3rd fret of E and A strings (G and C), on the 5th fret (A and D) and on the 7th fret (B and E) of the same strings. You'll use these notes quite often in the future because they're very useful as a reference point. Most songs use these notes and you can also use them as point of reference for navigating the fretboard, without always having to count steps from the open strings. Notice that the fret markers (dot-inlays) are on the same positions where these 6 key tones are, and they share a similar purpose.

Again, you can use mnemonics to better memorize these notes/tones. For example:

- 3 **G**rumpy **C**ats with 5 **A**ngry **D**onkeys scare 7 **B**ig **E**lephants.

This doesn't make any sense but hopefully you can do a better job than me. :) This way it is really easy to remember these key notes and know where they are at any given moment.

Next step on memorizing the entire fretboard is to be able to find almost instantly (with the help of the 6 key tones) all the notes on E and A strings.

Using octave shapes to find the notes

This is the next step in learning all notes and their positions on a guitar fingerboard. This is super important for mastering the guitar fretboard, and we'll look into this more in the 2nd book which will be out soon.

Now you can use <u>octave shapes</u> to find the notes on D, G, B, and high e strings quite fast. There are 4 octave shapes that I'm going to explain that are very useful for this.

1) Finding notes on the D string:

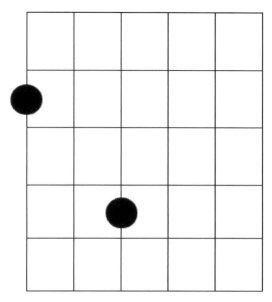

Octave shape #1

- If you play for example, G note on the 3rd fret of the E string, that same note, but an octave higher, can be found on the 5th fret of the D string. This applies to all the notes on the low E string.

2) Finding notes on the G string:

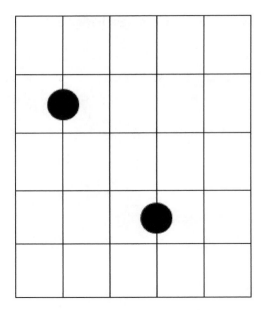

Octave shape #2

- For the notes on the G string we use the exact same shape but starting from an A string. For example - if you play C note on the 3rd fret A string, that same C (one octave higher) can be found on the 5th fret of the G string.

3) Finding notes on the B string:

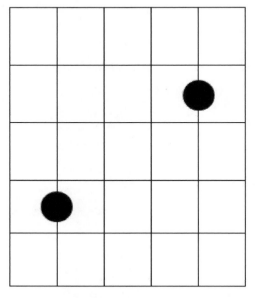

Octave shape #3

- Starting from an A string you can find the notes on a B string easily with the help of this shape. As an example, If you play the same C note again (3rd fret A string), that same C (also one octave higher) can be found on the 1st fret B string. Say you go to the 5th fret A string and you apply this shape, the D note will be found on the 3rd fret B string.

4) Finding notes on the high e string (Octave shape #4)

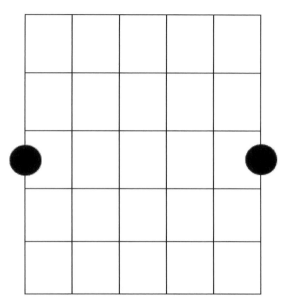

Octave shape #4

- This is the easiest shape simply because E and e strings are the same notes (but **two** octaves apart) and they share the same notes positions. If you already know the notes on the low E string, then you know the notes on the high 'e' as well. For example, the G note of the 3rd fret low E string is also found on the 3rd fret high e string.

After this, the next step is to memorize more key tones on D, G, B and e strings and do some specific exercises for memorizing all the notes. I won't get into that now simply because it is way beyond the scope of this book.

Just know that you'll eventually want to memorize every note on every fret, on all 6 guitar strings! This is not an easy task to do but you will get there as you gain experience. It must take some time.

This is a very important step for fretboard guitar mastery and the ability to play anything anywhere on a guitar fretboard. All musicians (piano players especially) have to learn the notes on their instrument, so trust me when I say that it's important, and hopefully it won't take so much time to learn after all the tricks I've shown you.

There are other aspects of fretboard mastery, but we'll deal with that in the 2nd book in the series.

How to read tablature

You have probably heard about tabs or tablature before but if you didn't let me explain what it is.

A tablature/tab is a simple way of writing down what is being played on guitar. It shows which note(s) is/are being played on which string(s) and fret(s). It is not meant to replace the standard musical notation by any means.

Being able to read written music (sight read) through notation is a valuable skill that is being taught in music schools. It is much harder to do on guitar than on other instruments like piano for example. It is not necessary for you as a guitar player to learn how to sight read, but it would be very useful to know how to read and write tabs in the beginning.

There are many famous and amazingly skillful guitar players who didn't invest time into learning how to sight read traditionally written music, and they didn't even bother to learn how. If you want to play classical music mainly, then learning how to sight read will be a must for you, especially if you want to go to a music school.

Beginners tend to rely on tablature a lot for finding out how to play certain songs, riffs, solos or melodies fast. Most experienced players and even some professional guitar players use tabs in order to quickly write down something (an exercise, a song idea, chord progression, lick, riff...) as it helps them remember it later.

- Here are the 2 examples of tab uses

Example 1 - Technique exercises (Chromatic scale)

```
e |-----------------------------------------------------5-6-7-8-9-|
B |-------------------------------------------4-5-6-7-8-----------|
G |-----------------------------------3-4-5-6-7------------------|
D |-------------------------2-3-4-5-6----------------------------|
A |-------------1-2-3-4-5----------------------------------------|
E |-0-1-2-3-4---------------------------------------------------|
```

In this example you can see a great technique exercise for a beginner. These kinds of exercises you'll often find written as tab because they are the easiest to write.

A scale is just a series of notes ordered in a specific way. This chromatic scale is not musical, it's meant to be played as an exercise for developing your left and right hand finger coordination, strength, dexterity and muscle memory. There are many other examples of this kind of exercises and you can make up your own too. More on this in a later section.

So how do we read this tab and play what is written? It's quite simple. We read the tab from left to right.

0 - is a symbol for an open string, meaning that the low E string you just play open, without any fingers holding it down.
1 - means that you put your finger on the 1st fret of whichever string the number is on, in this case on the low E. The same goes when you move to the A string and all other strings.

If the notes are at the same place but on different strings (one beneath the other), they should be played at the same time. This is how chords are usually written.

Example 2 - Chord tab

Tabs are also used to write down how chords are played.

You can often see something like this:

a) Tab - 022000

There are 6 numbers here. First number (from left to right) is for the low E string. In this case it's 0, meaning that you don't put any fingers on this string and you just play it open. Second number is for the A string - your finger goes on the 2nd fret A string. Third number is for the D string - so your finger goes to the 2nd fret D string. G, B and e strings are played open.

This is an E minor chord by the way. More on playing chords later in the book.

b) Tab - XX0232

The first X here means that the low E string is not played at all. The same goes for the A string. They should not be heard when you play this chord, so you just skip them and play the other strings. D string is played open and your fingers go to the 2nd fret G string, 3rd fret B and 2nd fret e. This is a D major chord.

Downsides to using tabs

In your first few years of playing you will probably come across a lot of tabs, especially online. Most of them are improvised in the way they are written. Their authors don't always make sense with their tab writing, so don't let them confuse you. Also, many song tabs are not accurate at all. You need to learn to trust your ears and use common sense with tabs. Always check with the actual song if it's right. Also make sure that you are playing it right.

There are many disadvantages to using tabs for learning to play music. Unlike traditional music notation, tabs only show **which** notes should be played. They don't show **how** the notes should be played - are they played slow or fast, do you let the notes sustain, do you use vibrato, is it loud or quiet, what is the note length, etc.

Another big disadvantage is that, unlike standard musical notation, tabs don't show the rhythm and notes length. They also don't show which fingers should be used for playing a chord, riff, lick, etc. All these elements are crucial if you want to play a great solo or an amazing melody line by learning or even reading it from the paper, and sound good at the same time.

That's why tabs are a good addition only to your practice and to help you remember the stuff that you already know. They are also great for writing specific left/right hand technique exercises designed for improving: speed, picking, coordination, control of the notes, etc.

In the end you should use tabs especially in the beginning and later on for your technique and writing your own songs, arrangements, etc, but try not to rely on them too much for learning songs, solos and melodies. There is a much better, more rewarding, but at the same time harder, way to do this. It's called **transcribing**, or figuring out everything by ear. I'll talk about transcribing at some other time, but know that it is the best way to learn any instrument and get the most benefits. And the more you do it the more you'll get better at it.

Finger names and how to read chord boxes

The chord boxes unlike tabs show you how the chord looks like, where to put the fingers on the fretboard and what strings to press in order to play that chord.

Here is an example of a chord box:

D minor, Tab - XX0231

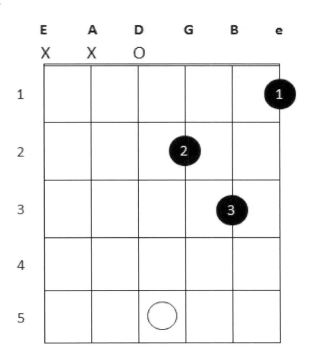

Vertical lines here represent the guitar strings and horizontal lines represent the frets. The double horizontal line at the top is a guitar nut.

X's mean that those strings should not be played, while "O" next to X means that the string is played open, as we've talked about before. The numbers on the left are for the frets, and the black filled circles show where your fingers should go.

The numbers in those black circles show the fingering, or which fingers are used to hold down that note.

When it comes to the <u>fretting hand</u> fingers (the one we play the notes on the neck with) we often use names like: index finger, middle finger, ring finger, pinky or little finger and thumb.

Your index finger is also your 1st finger, middle is your second, ring your third, pinky your 4th and thumb is just thumb or 'T'. :)

This means that for our chord example your 1st finger goes to the 1st fret high e string, your 2nd finger goes to the 2nd fret G string, and your 3rd finger goes to the 3rd fret B string. This is a D minor chord.

By the way, don't worry about playing these chords right now, we'll come back to them in the next chapter.

Pick versus fingers, and how to hold a guitar pick properly

When I first started learning to play I used my fingers exclusively for note picking and strumming. Holding the pick and trying to pick the notes and strum guitar with it felt very awkward. The sound I was getting with a pick was not good at all because of that.

That's why In my first month of learning how to play I used my thumb and my index finger for strumming, even though I've seen that almost everyone else plays with a pick. I wondered what was I doing wrong.

Later on I realized that there were some limitations to what I can do with my fingers. I didn't want to have long nails, and the sound I was getting was very soft and not loud enough. In spite of it feeling awkward I tried to learn to strum with a pick once again and to my surprise, I realized it was just a matter of getting used to playing with a pick with the right technique.

Now don't get me wrong, playing fingerstyle (without a pick) is very powerful and awesome way to play anything on guitar. But for starters it's best to get used to playing with a pick because it'll be easier, believe it or not. After some time when you get all the basics down on guitar and build up your foundations, you can move into the fingerstyle world if you want.

Fingerstyle is very complex and particularly good for playing chords and melody at the same time, arranging songs in an interesting way (all instruments in one), and having your guitar sound like a complete one-man band. Take a look at the guitar players like Chet Atkins, Tommy Emmanuel, Jeff Beck, Igor Presnyakov, Sungha Jung, Mark Knopfler, and you will be amazed at what they can do.

There is also the **hybrid style technique** where you use both a pick and your middle and ring fingers at the same time. This is the style I personally use most of the time because it gives me with the most versatility in my playing, and it suits my style. The only disadvantage to the hybrid style is that you have one less finger available for playing notes, since index finger along with the thumb is busy holding the pick.

No matter what style you choose, like I said, you should start with a pick first, so here are a few images showing the best and proper way to hold a pick.

1) To get the best pick position first place the pick on the side of your index finger with its tip pointed at the same direction as the finger.

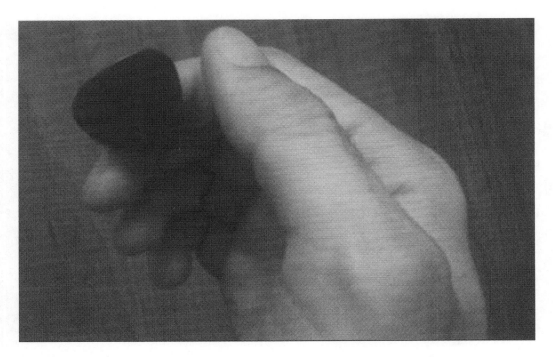

2) Then place your thumb on the pick but make sure that the pick is sticking out on the side of the thumb, around the 90 degree angle.

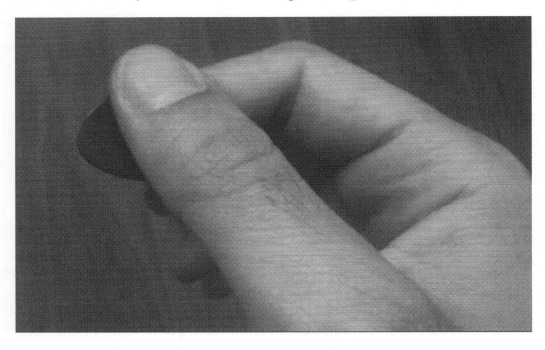

3) This is how it looks like from the other side

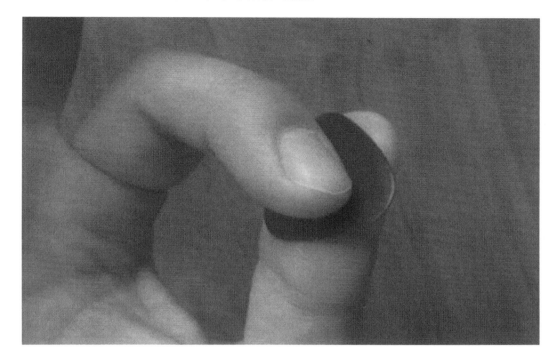

A couple of important pointers:

- Make sure that you're not holding the pick too firmly because you will tense up and that is going to show in your playing; also don't hold it too loosely because the pick might slip out of your hand or move to the side.

- When you down-strum with a pick the tip of your index finger shouldn't be hitting the strings before the pick accidentally. I had a problem with this as it became a bad habit of mine, and I had to work hard on correcting it.

- When you're strumming or picking make sure that the pick is just slightly angled toward the strings, like shown here:

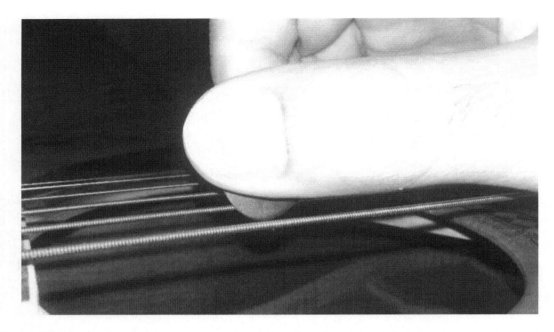

This will make it easier to strum and avoid the bad habit I just mentioned.

How to hold a guitar and correct body posture

Many people overlook the importance of the correct body posture while playing/practicing guitar. It used to happen to me constantly that after a long playing session I felt an ache in my back muscles and my shoulder. That's not good. Even today I still have to remind myself how to hold a guitar in a way that doesn't put strain on my back, shoulders and neck, and sit properly.

While playing or practicing your body should be relaxed. As much as possible try not to tense your muscles because it won't produce good results. Correct posture is important as it can prevent back and shoulder pain, and prevent you from developing bad habits in your playing.

There are a couple of ways to hold a guitar, either while sitting down or while standing up. Most of your practice will be done while sitting so that is recommended at the beginning. You can get accustomed to playing while standing up later (it will take some time).

Make sure that you sit on an armless chair or on a place where nothing can obstruct your playing. You can learn to play either in a classical position or in a standard position. If you want to play classical music and become a classical guitar player then you should obviously play in a classical position. I assume that most of you will want to learn the standard position, so that is what I'm going to explain.

- How to do it

Sit down and place the guitar in a way so that its curvy part rests on your right leg (or left leg if you're left-handed). Make sure that the bottom of the neck is parallel to the floor, and that the upper back edge region of the guitar body touches/leans on your stomach/chest area.

Make sure that the thickest string on guitar is the string closest to your face, and that the thinnest string is the one closest to the floor.

Your back should be straight and relaxed, and not curved and hunched over a guitar. This is a very common mistake people make. I had a problem with this too because when I wasn't hunched over I could barely see the fingerboard and what I

53

was playing. The trick is to just tilt the guitar toward your face slightly so that you can see the fretboard a little bit better, while keeping your back and shoulders straight and relaxed.

Your **fretting hand** is your left hand if you're right-handed. It's the hand that presses the strings between the frets on a guitar fingerboard. Your **strumming hand** is your right hand if you're right-handed. It's the hand which holds the pick and strums the chords.

The elbow of your fretting hand should be at a 90 degree angle and free to move left and right across the guitar neck while your shoulder is neutral. The thumb of the fretting hand should rest/lean on the back of the guitar neck, with the rest of your fretting hand fingers curled slightly in their knuckles and resting on the guitar strings.

It's important to make sure that your fretting hand is not supporting/holding the weight of the guitar neck!

Your strumming hand should be going over the guitar body with the region on the inside of your arm (where the elbow is), resting on the top right corner/edge of the body (top left if it's a left-handed guitar). Note that with an electric guitar, or any other guitar which is smaller in size (or with thinner body), your picking hand elbow will not lean against the body of a guitar but it will rather hang in the air - which is normal, but you may need to experiment a bit to find the most comfortable position.

Chapter 3 - Learning guitar chords

Finally, we're ready to learn some guitar chords. Most of the chords we are going to learn are called "basic open chords". That's because we use open strings along with some fretted notes to play them. You should think of these chords as your lifelong friends. They're always going to be there and you're going to use them a lot. ;)

Like I said before, a scale is just a series of notes ordered in a specific (scale formula) way, and Chords are built from scales. We won't go into that in this book.

There are <u>many</u> different types of chords. To give you an idea, there are: major, minor, sus2, sus4, augmented, diminished, 6th's, minor 6, major 7, dominant 7, minor 7, minor 7b5, diminished 7 (full diminished), augmented 7, add9, 11's,13's... Plus there are: power chords (5ths), slash chords, 1st, 2nd and 3rd chord inversions, altered chords... Like that is not enough, all these chords can be played in 5 different shapes on guitar (also known as the CAGED system).

I mean, the list is enormous (this is not even the whole list) and sounds complex and confusing, but my goal is not to confuse you or scare you away. Once you understand the basic chord theory it is not that hard to learn all these types of chords. There is a way to explain how all this works and applies on guitar and it is actually quite easy to understand! This is the topic that I'll deal with in the next book, again sorry for another plug. :)

Here we will just focus on the practical aspects of learning your first 15 guitar chords to get you started.

3 main types of chords

I know that this goes against what I explained just a moment ago but bear with me for a second here. :)

Before learning the basic chords, I must explain first that in the essence, there are 3 main types of chords that all other types belong to (with the exception of the sus2/4 and power chords). Those are:

1. Major

2. Minor

3. Dominant.

This is a very simple chord breakdown. The reason for that is because of their sound by which you can distinguish them more or less easily and their function in a chord progression

- major chords are happy and upbeat sounding,

- minor chords are sad sounding,

- dominant chords are a bit dissonant and create/add tension in a song.

In this book I'm going to show you how to play the basic major and minor chords, and some open dominant chords that are used very often in songs.

How to learn and practice the basic guitar chords

When you see the shape of the chord try to form that shape on guitar with your fingers. It's going to be very difficult to form these chords, simply because your fingers are not used to it. That's why we're starting with the easiest chords to form first, and then we're progressively moving onto more difficult chords to play. You will get them all eventually!

After you can form the chord, play each note of the chord with your picking hand separately. Go all the way down, then all the way up.

Make sure that you don't mute any of the strings, and that each of the fretted notes (the notes that you hold with your fingers) have a clear sound.

If any of your fingers that are holding the chord notes just gently touch the string above or lean over any of the strings below, in any way, those strings won't be heard when you play them - they will be muted. So make sure that you do not mute any of the strings with your fingers! It is easier said than done, I know, but you'll get it with practice.

Also, your fingers need to be closer to the fretwires toward the bridge (horizontal lines on the chord box) when gripping chords or individual notes on guitar. Try not to put them in the middle of the fret because it will be very hard or even impossible to get a clear note to ring out. Likewise, if you don't apply enough pressure on a note that you're holding, it will be muted or you won't get a clear note sound.

There are many possible finger combinations for the following chords(which finger to use for which fret). I'm going to show the best ones to learn for beginners.

For each of the following chords I'll also show you the tab, how it looks in a chord box, what fingers to place where, and I'll give you some tips for playing them in a best way.

Basic Minor Chords

E minor (can also be written as E min, or Em)

This is one of the easiest chords that you're going to learn, hence why we're starting with this one. Here's the tab:

Tab - 022000

- The chord looks like this:

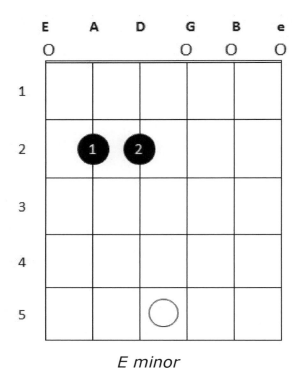

E minor

To play this chord simply put your index finger on the 2nd fret of the A string, and your middle finger on the 2nd fret D string. The rest of the strings are played open.

This chord is pretty straightforward. Make sure that you do not mute the strings G, B and e with your middle finger and the low E string with your index.

A minor

Tab - x02210

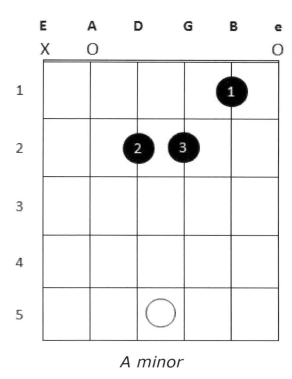

A minor

This is another very easy chord to learn but it requires three fingers. To play this chord put your index finger on the 1st fret B string, middle on the 2nd fret D string and ring finger on the 2nd fret G string. Low E string should not be played and A and e are played open.

You can mute the low E string by reaching over with the thumb and just gently touching it, or you can just simply avoid playing it altogether.

D minor

Tab - xx0231

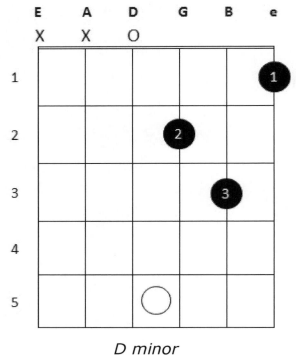

D minor

Put your index finger on the 1st fret e string, middle on the 2nd fret G string and your ring finger on the 3rd fret B string.

Again, you can mute the E and A strings by reaching over with your thumb. This is easier if you have large hands, but not that important. It's enough to just consciously avoid playing them for this chord.

Basic Major Chords

Now we move on to major chords. The three chords that we learned so far were minor. You'll notice that with these types of chords the sound is happy, positive and upbeat.

E Major (can also be written as E maj, or just E. This applies to any major chord)

Tab - 022100

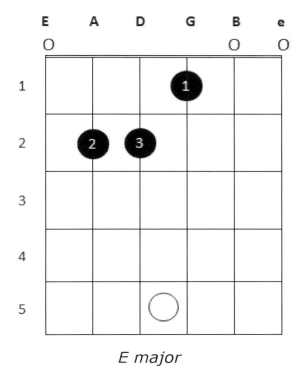

E major

Notes that are used are the same as for the E min chord with the one only difference of adding the note on the 1st fret G string. Fingering is also different a bit.

Your index finger goes to the 1st fret G string, middle to the 2nd fret A string, ring finger to the 2nd fret D string. The rest of the strings are played open as showed on the above diagram.

If you learned E min, E major will be very easy too. After you learn them both try to play one after the other and you'll hear how only one note makes a big difference to the sound - the difference between major and minor!

A major

Tab - x02220

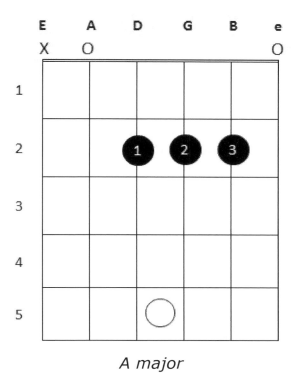

A major

Put your index on the 2nd fret D string, middle on the 2nd fret G string, ring on the 2nd fret B string. A and high e are played open.

This chord can be a little bit trickier than the rest. Namely because your index finger is far from the fretwire because of the other fingers, making the note to sound properly difficult. While you might not get it at first, you will with get it with regular practice.

When compared to the A min can you notice which note has changed? The difference between major and minor chords is in one note semitone only!

D major

Tab - xx0232

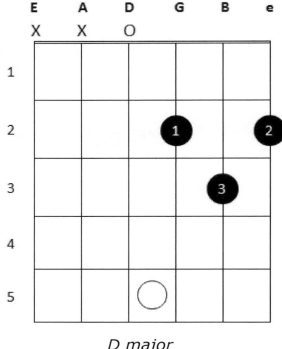

D major

Index finger goes to the 2nd fret G string, middle to the 2nd fret high e string and ring finger to the 3rd fret B string. D string is played open, and E - A strings shouldn't be played.

It can be hard at first to get the high e string to sound correctly because your ring finger on the B string can mute it easily. Like with D minor, you can reach over with your thumb to mute the thickest 2 strings.

When you practice all these chords it's imperative that you play them as clearly and cleanly as possible. Always strive to avoid mistakes. We will get to how to practice these chords in a bit.

G major

Tab - 320003

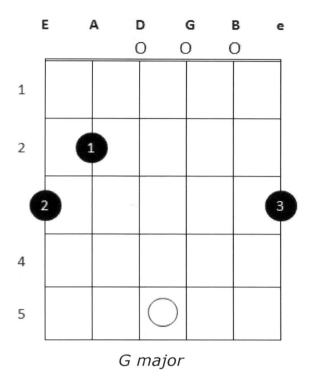

G major

Index goes to the 2nd fret A string, middle 3rd fret low E string, ring - 3fret high e string. D, G and B strings are played open.

This is your G chord which you'll use quite a lot. There are some variations to playing this chord with different finger combinations, but you should learn to use this one first. Be careful not to mute the A string with your middle finger.

C major

Tab - x32010

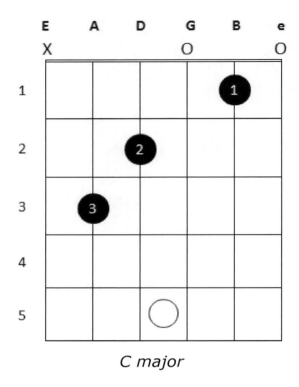

C major

   Index - 1st fret B string, Middle - 2nd fret D string, Ring - 3rd fret A string. G and e strings are played open and low E should not be played.

   Try not to mute the high e string with your index finger and the G string with your middle finger.

   C chord requires a bit of a finger stretch but it is quite doable. I'll share with you the best finger stretching exercise after this section.

Basic Dominant 7th Chords

Now we're moving into the 7th chord territory. First thing to note is their difference in sound.

A7 (or A dominant 7, or A dom7)

Tab - x02020

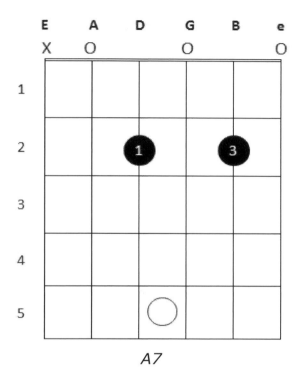

A7

To play the A7 chord all you have to do is form the normal A chord but remove the middle finger and play the G string open.

It can be very hard not to mute the G string with this finger placement. That's why I recommend that you try the following fingering: put your middle finger on the 2nd fret D string, and your ring finger on the 2nd fret B. This is an easier way to play this chord and not mute the G string, but nonetheless it will require some practice to get your middle two fingers to move in this way.

How does A7 sound to you? It's one of the most used chord in blues along with E7 and D7. After you can play this chord, make sure that you play A, Am and A7, and compare their sound. Notice the difference - happy, sad, bluesy/tension maker.

E7

Tab - 020100

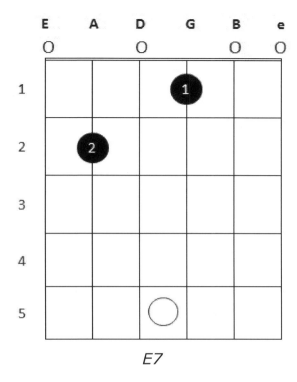

E7

Similarly to A7, all you have to do in order to play E7 is to form the E chord on guitar and lift off your ring finger, and play the D string open. This shouldn't give you any problems.

There is a very much used variation of this chord - when you add the note on the 3rd fret B string with your little finger. This one note enhances the 'dominant 7th' sound of the chord. Give it a try, just know that it will require some practice to stretch your fingers in awkward positions like that.

C7

Tab - x32310

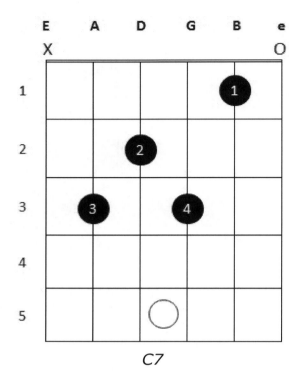

C7

    This is the first chord so far that requires the use of 4 fingers. All you have to do is form the regular C shape and add the note on the 3rd fret G string with your little finger. Once you learn the C chord, C7 won't be very difficult.

D7

Tab - xx0212

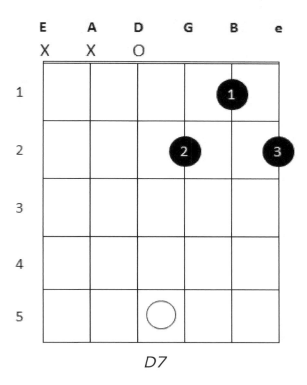

D7

This one is interesting. It looks like a regular D chord but in reverse. Fingering is also different. Your index goes to the 1st fret B string, middle 2nd fret G and ring finger to the 3rd fret high e string. Still not too difficult.

G7

Tab - 320001

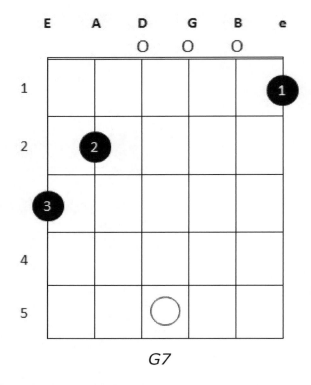

G7

This one is a little bit tricky mainly because you really need to be able to stretch your fingers enough to get that note on the high e string. Your index goes to the 1st fret high e, middle 2nd fret A, ring 3rd fret E string. Make sure that you do stretching exercises that I'll give you in the next section.

B7

Tab - x21201

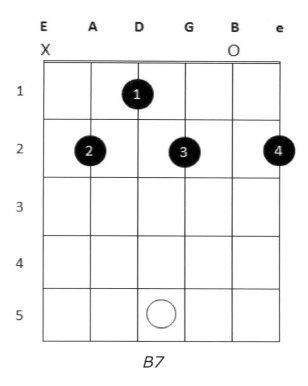

B7

This is another chord that is used in blues very often. Out of all the chords so far, this one will require more time and practice to get used to. It is a very cool sounding chord.

As for the fingering, index goes to the 1st fret D string, middle 2nd fret A, ring 2nd fret G and pinky 2nd fret high e string. B string is open, you'll need to practice the positioning of your fingers in way that you don't mute it.

Introduction to barre chords

F major

Tab - 133211

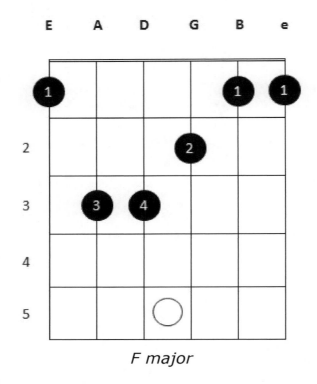

F major

   F major chord is the first chord here that is not an open chord, but a *barre chord*, meaning that you have to play more than one note with one of your fingers. In the case of F, it's your index finger. If this sounds confusing, bear with me for a second.

   This chord is technically much harder to learn than the open chords we've talked about so far, and in that regard it is more advanced. It requires tremendous finger strength which is only gained slowly through consistent practice.

   In order to play it, you have to put your index finger across the 1st fret and press down the strings as hard as you can. You've just barred the 1st fret with your index (hence the name: barre chord). Make sure that you're barring the 1st fret with the side of your index finger (its fleshy part) and you can use your middle finger as a support. It should look like this:

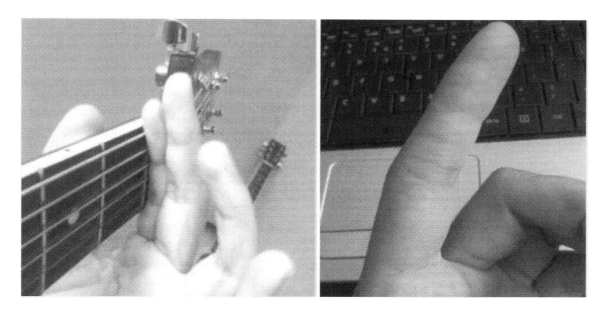

Now try to play each string. All of the strings should ring out cleanly without any muffled notes. If this is too hard (and it will be) try to move your index to the 5th fret. It should be easier there, but very hard still. Practice this for a while and when you get it right, gradually as you build finger strength work your way back to the 1st fret.

This is an excellent way to build up the necessary finger grip strength because it prepares you for the barre chords.

When you're ready, add the middle finger to the 2nd fret G string, ring to the 3rd fret A string, your little finger to the 3rd fret D string, with your index barring the 1st fret. Easy right? ;) In any case, you shouldn't try to learn this chord before learning the open chords.

Many of the songs that you're going to learn use the F chord. There are a few variations of F that are easier to play, and they can be used as a substitute for the full F in a song.

The "Little F" and "Fmaj7" chords.

With the little F (Tab - xx3211) you have to bar only the thinnest two strings on the 1st fret, your middle finger goes to the 2nd fret G string, and your ring to the

3rd fret D string. E and A strings are not played (or muted). This is just a slightly easier way to play the F chord.

You can also use the Fmaj7 chord (Tab - xx3210) which is an even more easier way to play F, but know that it won't always fit in a song because it contains a note (functioning as maj7) that might not belong to the song's key. In other words, it might not sound good. Not to confuse you any further, always remember the rule - **If it sounds good, it is good!**

You play this chord the same way as little F, but instead of barring the e and B strings, just place your index on the B string and leave the high e open. This is the F maj7, a chord with unique and dreamy sound.

If Fmaj7 is not sounding good in a song, you can just mute the thinnest e string and play the super simplified F chord:

Tab - xx321x.

This is the easiest way to play the F chord but the strings with X's on them have to be muted. This won't sound as full the whole F major, but you can still use it and it will sound good. It will do the job. :)

B minor

Tab - x24432

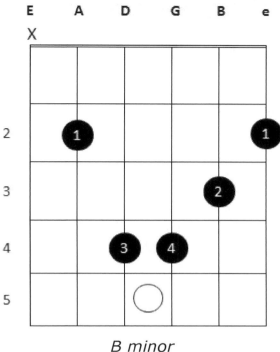

B minor

This is another very common chord in songs. It is a barre chord, but it's also a little bit easier than F.

Your index finger covers the 2nd fret A string and the 2nd fret high E string, middle goes to the 3rd fret B string, ring to the 4th fret D, and your little finger goes to the 4th fret G string.

Also, if it's too hard you can play it like this: Tab - x2443x, but make sure that the thinnest string is properly muted with your index finger.

B major

Tab - x24442

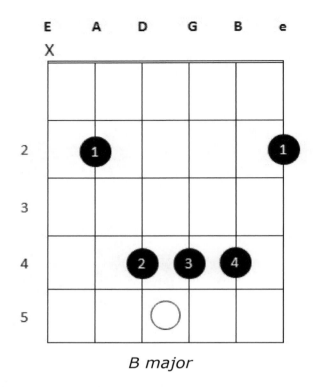

B major

This is the hardest chord so far! I remember I struggled with this chord for a while (several months). Some people get it faster than others, while some struggle. In any case, I'm going to show the best and easiest ways to play this chord so that you do not struggle with it as much as I did.

To play it, you have to bar the strings A and high e on the 2nd fret with your index finger, and with the rest of your fingers you have to play the same shape as that of an A chord - middle finger: 4th fret D string, ring: 4th fret G and little: 4th fret B.

Alternatively, you can bar the strings on the 4th fret with your ring finger. This is the way that I play it today but some people prefer the first way. Some can even bar the D, G and B strings with their little finger. It depends on your hand physiology. I know that almost all serious players use their ring finger to bar the mentioned strings, so that is the one I would advise you to work on.

In any way, in order to correctly play this chord your fingers need to be strengthened and you need to work on your hand stretching exercises. I'm going to show you those in the next section.

There are a couple of easier ways to use this chord in a song even if you still cannot play the whole. The first one is:

Tab - xx4442, or even easier - xx444x

With the first shape just leave out the 2nd fret A string note and don't play it, just place the tip of your index on the 2nd fret high e string. Or you can just play the A chord on the 4th fret, but it's very important to make sure that the unwanted strings are muted. Otherwise, it will sound horrible. :)

This is a chord inversion by the way, but don't worry about that for now. What matters is that these two shapes will sound good in songs that use the B chord!

Another easier way to play B chord is:

Tab - x2x44x

This is still a regular B chord (not an inevrsion) - index plays the 2nd fret A, and ring/pinky play the 4th fret G/B. You just have to make sure that the D string is muted with your index finger just leaning over it. I use this shape often in song arrangements because it's very practical.

Finger strength and stretching exercises

Learning to play all these chords and using them in songs is going to require that you build up your finger strength, dexterity and muscle memory. Also, your fingers will need to develop new stretching capabilities in order to play any of the chords.

I'm going to share with you 2 extensive exercises - one for developing finger strength, and one for finger stretching. All you need for them is a guitar.

Note that with these exercises your fretting hand will become sore and you will feel muscle pain (like when you workout), but there is a difference between a 'good' pain and a 'bad' pain. A good pain is when you feel soreness in your muscles during or after the workout, while bad pain is a way that your body's telling you that something's wrong!

Please make sure that you listen to your body and know your limits! If you feel that kind of a bad pain, simply stop! If the pain persists when you come back to it after a week or so, please see a doctor.

I Finger strength workout

This exercise, or a workout if you will, is going to require that you use the techniques called **hammer on** and **pull off**.

A hammer on is a guitar technique where you play the note on guitar just by slamming your fingertip on a note that you wish to play (hence the name - hammer on).

For example - put your index finger on the 1st fret B string and play it with a pick. You can play the note on the 2nd fret of the same string just by *hammering it on* with your middle finger; or in other words, by hitting it with its fingertip. This is a very useful technique and it's used quite a lot in guitar playing.

A pull off is an opposite movement. It's when you play a note with a pick and then simply 'pull off' the note by lifting your finger off. Doing that will result (if you do it correctly) in hearing a new note that you pulled off to.

For example - put your index finger on the 1st fret B string and play it with a pick. Then simply *pull off* your index finger by lifting it off from the string in a way that the B note (open B string) is heard loud and clear (at the same volume as the note that you picked). Another example - put your index on the 1st fret B and middle to the 2nd fret B, and play the 2nd fret B with a pick. Then pull off the middle so that the note on the 1st fret B is heard.

You can do hammer on's and pull off's on guitar between any of your fingers and frets that are within their reach, in any position on any string. The sound and a feel that you get by using these is a little bit different than what you would get if you played a note with a pick. They sound a lot more smoother when played in a sequence. They are awesome for developing finger strength.

Before working on your finger strength you need to come to grips with your hammer on's and pull off's and be able to perform them correctly.

- Here's is how to get started working on your finger strength.

Finger strength exercise #1

```
e | -5h6h7h8-------------------------------------------- |
B | ---------5h6h7h8----------------------------------- |
G | ----------------5h6h7h8---------------------------- |
D | -----------------------5h6h7h8-------------------- |
A | ------------------------------5h6h7h8---------- |
E | ----------------------------------------5h6h7h8- |
```

- Place your index finger on the 5th fret of the high e string and play it with a pick. Then hammer on (low 'h' letter in tab) with your middle finger the note on the 6th fret of the same string. Then do the same with your ring finger and your little finger on 7th and 8th frets.

- Do these exercise all the way up to the low E string, and then do it again all the way down to the high e.

- Continue going back and forth for 2.5 minutes at least. Then move on to the exercise #2.

Finger strength exercise #2

```
e | -8p7p6p5 - - - - - - - - - - - - - - - - - - - - - - - - - - - - - - - - - - - - - - - - - - - - - - |
B | - - - - - - - - -8p7p6p5 - - - - - - - - - - - - - - - - - - - - - - - - - - - - - - - - - - - - - - |
G | - - - - - - - - - - - - - - - -8p7p6p5 - - - - - - - - - - - - - - - - - - - - - - - - - - - - - - - |
D | - - - - - - - - - - - - - - - - - - - - - - -8p7p6p5 - - - - - - - - - - - - - - - - - - - - - - - - |
A | - - - - - - - - - - - - - - - - - - - - - - - - - - - - - -8p7p6p5 - - - - - - - - - - |
E | - - - - - - - - - - - - - - - - - - - - - - - - - - - - - - - - - - - - - -8p7p6p5 - |
```

- Now we're going in reverse. Place your little finger on the 8th fret high e, and your ring, middle and index on the 7th, 6th and 5th frets. Play the 8th fret with a pick and then pull off (letter 'p' on tab) to the note on the 7th fret that your ring finger is holding. Pull off again to the 6th fret and then to the 5th fret.

- Do these for each of the strings like shown on tab. Go all the way up to the low E and then all the way down to high e.

- Do this exercise also for 2.5 minutes at least.

Finger strength exercise #3

After these 2 exercises the next step would be to combine the two. Start on the high e string on any fret that you choose (just know that as you move towards the nut frets get larger and this exercise becomes harder to do - which is good!).

Essentially, start as in exercise #1 (on any fret) on high e string, and then after you hammer on to the 8th fret pull off right away to the 7th. You would play with a pick only the first note of the sequence on each string.

Same as before, go all the way up and all the way down, and do this for 2.5 minutes. It is going to be really hard! That's why I would advise you to first start with 2 and 3 finger combinations that I'll explain next.

Pulling off is a bit harder than hammering on as it's hard to get the note to ring out at high enough volume. You will get them both with consistent practice!

In order to perform this exercise correctly you need make sure that you follow these guidelines:

1) All notes that you play need to be equal, meaning that the volume is relatively the same. If you want to play super fast passages like Joe Satriani does, it's vital that you try your best to keep the note volume even and that each note is clear, smooth, and heard loud enough.

2) Make sure that you do not angle your fretting hand fingers to the fretboard while doing this, but rather keep them perpendicular to the frets as much as possible. This will help you practice the best hand position for playing fast sequences with good technique.

3) Use your fingertips. Either for pulling off or hammering down, it's important that you use your fingertips to get the best sound and practice the best finger placement for playing fast stuff later in your playing.

4) Regularity here is key. All it takes is 5-10 minutes a day to spend on this exercises, and it will do wonders for your technique and finger strength.

5) Do not ignore bad pain. If it persists after taking a break make sure that you see a doctor. Soreness is fine though. When you feel it, make sure that you stop for 5 seconds or so and then continue with the exercise.

2 and 3-finger combinations

These exercises (4-finger combinations) are too hard to begin with, but you can build up to them by using less fingers in a combination. You would first start with the easier - 2 finger combinations, then move on to 3 finger combinations, and then to 4 finger combinations that are shown in the previous examples.

- If you number your fretting hand fingers like this:

Index finger - 1

Middle finger - 2

Ring finger - 3

Little finger - 4

- Recommended 2 finger combinations to start with are:

a) 1-2, 1-3, 1-4;

> Hammer on's

b) 2-3; 2-4; 3-4;

c) 4-3; 4-2; 4-1;

> Pull off's

d) 3-2; 3-1; 2-1;

- Choose a finger combination to practice (you should do them all)

- Pick any fret (I usually advise to begin on the 5th fret and work your way to the nut),

- start on the high e string,

- always pick the first note in a sequence with a pick,

- go all the way up to low E and then all the way down to high e string.

- You can also practice your index finger pulling off to an open string.

   You should also combine hammer on's and pulls off's in a sequence. For example: 1-2-1; 1-3-1; 1-4-1;

   After you get good at this, you can move on to 3-finger combinations. Recommended 3-finger combinations (if the number is going up - it's a hammer on, and if it's going down - it's a pull off):

a) 1-2-3; 2-3-4; 1-2-4; 1-3-4;

b) 3-2-1; 4-3-2; 4-3-1; 4-2-1;

c) 1-3-2; 1-4-3; 1-4-2; 2-4-3;

   After you get good at these as well, you can move on to 4-finger combinations for which I already gave you the exercises. You can even make your own patterns and get creative with this as much as you want.

   It is very important that you try as many different combinations as possible. Doing so will give you tremendous finger strength, dexterity and coordination.

You will also grip chords much easier - that dreaded F chord barre is going to become a breeze if you practice this enough.

II Finger stretching workout

Playing chords correctly often requires that we really stretch out our fretting hand fingers in ways we haven't stretched them before. This exercise is going to help you with that; the whole point of it is that you practice stretching your fingers on guitar and improve your reach, as well as strength and dexterity.

Make sure that your hand and fingers are perpendicular to the fretboard and not angled in any way. Your fingers also need to stay on the frets as you play the notes.

As you move from low E to the high e string your fingers will get more and more curled up in their knuckles.

- The exercise looks like this:

Frets	7	8	9	10	11	12
Ex.1			index	middle	ring	pinky
Ex.2	index	middle	ring	pinky		
Ex.3		index	middle	ring		pinky
Ex.4	index		middle	ring	pinky	
Ex.5	index		middle	ring		pinky

- Here is how you must perform this exercise:

1) You'll need to do the Examples 1 to 5 starting from the low E string and move down all the way to the high e. As the table shows, put your index finger on the 9th fret (low E string) and play the note with a pick. Then put your middle/ring/pinky finger on frets: 10/11/12, and play each note that you put your fingers on.

2) After you play the Ex.1 sequence on the E string, just move your fingers down to A string and play the same sequence. Continue doing this all the way to the high e.

3) Then do the Ex.2 from the low E string again but starting from the 7th fret with your index finger... Just follow the table and do the same as with Ex.1.

4) In Ex. 3 you'll need to stretch out your pinky to the 12th fret.

5) In Ex 4. you are stretching your index and your middle finger.

6) Example 5 is the hardest because it requires that you stretch both index-middle and ring-pinky fingers at the same time.

Practicing these examples will make you feel soreness in your muscles, but if you feel any 'bad' kind of pain, please stop! Try again after some time, but if the pain persists go see a doctor.

You shouldn't spend too much time on this exercise - 5 minutes is optimal. It's important that you do not overdo it.

Always practice smart and safe!

As you get good in this position (from the 7th fret), move everything down one step to the 5th fret and repeat the whole exercise. It will be harder because gaps between the frets are larger and they will require that you put more stretch.

As you get good you can move by one fret all the way down toward guitar nut. When you get to the 1st fret that would be the hardest position because gaps between the frets there are the largest.

Best exercise to master the chord changes

Once you're able to hold at least 2-3 chords and play them without any muted strings or unwanted string noise, the next big challenge is to learn how to change between one chord to another fast enough so that you can keep the pace and play a song without stopping - while sounding clear at the same time.

There is an excellent game/exercise for this, and its called "*1 minute chord changes*". I'll explain how it is done.

Choose two chords that you want to master the changes for, and time yourself for 1 minute. You need some sort of a timer device for this or a simple clock. You can also find a timer online. I just use a timer on my phone.

The game is very simple - you need to make as many changes as you can between two chords that you choose, but you need to keep in mind the following rules and guidelines:

1. The chords should sound clear without any muted strings, unwanted string noise, muffled notes, etc. It's OK if the chord is not perfect sometime, you can still count it. The point is to get your fingers to move fast and precise, but you should strive to make the chords sounding good.

2. The change doesn't count if a chord is not sounding clear enough. Be your own judge on that and be honest with yourself. There is no point in cheating.

3. Use one quick down strum for both chords. The focus here is on your fretting hand entirely.

4. "**The shortest distance between two points is a straight line**". This means that in order to master the chord changes and play them as fast as possible, you need to eliminate any finger movements that are redundant. For example, switching between Amin and Emaj is just a simple up and down movement with your fingers.

You need to identify the shortest distances between any two chords that you practice and make your fingers move in this way. This is not as hard as it might seem at first!

5. Every time you change the chord you should make your count. For example, C to G is 1, G to C - 2, C to G - 3, G to C - 4, etc.

6. After 1 minute expires write down how many changes you've made. This is a very good motivational trick because with time you'll be able to watch yourself as

you improve and become better at this. The number of changes will go up. You should compete with yourself and try to make more changes the next time you practice. This is another really good reason to keep a practice journal.

When you first start trying to do these 1 minute chord changes you'll probably get around 5 or more! Don't worry about how long it takes you to make one change, you're going to really struggle with them at first! With little time and practice you'll develop a muscle memory and your fingers will automatically go where they're supposed to without you thinking about that.

7. Your goal at this stage should be 30 'good' changes before moving on to the next two chords. After a few years of playing you'll be able to make 100+ changes in one minute! As you get faster and faster it might not be possible to strum the whole chords, it's ok then to strum just a few thickest strings.

It's amazing how this simple exercise works well. It is the fastest way to master any chord change on guitar! With enough practice these chords will become so much automated that you'll be able to play them in your sleep, instantly, with your eyes closed, or while talking or watching a movie at the same time!

As you master guitar chords and the changes, they will become a part of you and you'll never be able to forget them! How cool is that? :)

Chapter 4 - Working on your strumming skills

For playing guitar it's obviously not enough to learn just the chords and the changes, you need to learn how to strum them too, and be able to play a song. This is probably even more important than the chords themselves! You can make great music just by playing around with one or two notes and using different rhythms.

Do you want to know one of the little known 'secrets' to sounding great on guitar or any other instrument? It's the rhythm skills. That's what makes a guitar player sound great. It goes without saying that you really need to work on your rhythm skills and develop a strong sense of timing.

In this chapter we're going to focus on developing your strumming technique and some of your rhythm skills. By rhythm skills I mean: a strong sense of timing, the use of dynamics in playing, phrasing, accents, the ability to play with strumming patterns, syncopation, odd time meters, etc. It all relates to the 'feel' in your playing a lot.

Understanding time signatures

In this part I'm going to explain some basics of the rhythm theory. This is important not just for the exercises that I'm going to show you later, but for everything else that is related to rhythm guitar playing. Every guitar player needs to know this if he/she wants to understand rhythm and time, and truly sound good. Basic rhythm is not that hard to understand but it can be confusing. I'm going to explain it as best as I can.

We all had to learn how to tap and count rhythm at some point in our school music classes. I'm going to briefly explain something similar again, and more importantly, we're going to see how it applies on guitar.

If you've ever looked at a sheet music before (traditional music notes written on a paper for a particular music piece), you might have noticed that there are numbers written at the beginning of the staff, for example 4/4 (one 4th is beneath the other)

This is called a **time signature** and understanding it can be really confusing and frustrating sometimes for many people. I know I struggled to understand it a lot.

When you see:

4
4

at the beginning of the staff, it means that there are 4 quarter notes in one bar. But wait, what is a bar you might ask?

A bar is a unit of time in which the music is divided. It is one complete cycle of the beats (or pulses - it's what we tap our hands or nod our heads to), and it's defined by the time signature. They help keeping the music organized into smaller chunks.

Time signature defines how many beats make up the rhythm or a groove of the song. In the previous 4/4 example, top 4 tells us there are 4 beats in a bar, and bottom 4 tells us the value of each beat. In this case it's a quarter note. So having 4/4 means that there are four quarter notes in one bar. Having 6/8 (another common time signature) means that there are 6 eight notes in one bar.

I know that this must be very confusing to you, but when you start practicing on guitar it will make more sense. Don't worry about this too much. Most of your practice at the beginning will be focused on 4/4 time and you're going to see how easy it is to play in 4/4.

How to strum a guitar

For many people, learning how to strum a guitar properly and develop a great sense of timing is very tricky. We've already discussed the ways you can strum a guitar (either with a pick or with fingers), and that if you're a beginner you should start learning with a pick first.

First and foremost, take your flat pick in the way I've described in some of the previous sections and try to strum a guitar. Does it feel strange or awkward? It's normal if it does.

When you strum a guitar it's important to be aware of the angle that your strumming hand hits or 'attacks' the strings. The strumming motion of your hand must not be perpendicular to the strings but rather just slightly angled. This is really important! (like shown on picture in 'how to hold a pick' section)

The strumming motion should come from your elbow and a little bit from your wrist), so you'll naturally strum at a slight angle (10-15 degrees) to the strings. As you strum faster and faster it becomes more of a wrist motion - like you're trying to shake off the water from your hand.

Before I start explaining the best exercise for strumming, there is one golden rule you need to follow when strumming a guitar:

Your strumming hand needs to be relaxed and you need to always keep it moving continuously down and up when you play.

Your hand can't be stiff or tensed up because it's going to show in your playing. In order to play in a relaxed way you need to feel the beat of the groove with your whole body and your strumming hand will relax and follow the beat naturally. It will move in an effortless motion - down and up. The best way to feel the beat is to start tapping your foot, nod your head and move your body along with the beat of the song.

Make sure that you don't hold your pick too tightly or too loosely, but with just the right amount of pressure. You're going to need to experiment with that to see exactly just how much pressure you need for optimal strumming.

The best way to practice strumming and get used to it, is to simply - strum.

What an amazing advice! :) But that's what this exercise is all about. I'm going to share with you a very powerful exercise that is going to do wonders to your timing and strumming technique. Strumming is one of the most important basic building blocks and it will allow you to play songs.

The strumming exercise is in 4/4 time. It's extensive, progressive and very effective, so make sure that you follow what I say closely, step by step.

Strumming exercise part 1 - Using only down-strums

1. Take your metronome and set the beat to 60 bpm. If you don't have one you can use a free one online. Just type in 'metronome' in the search engine.

Use your fretting hand to cover and mute guitar strings but do not press them against the fretboard. Now strum a guitar using a down-strum. You shouldn't hear any note when you strum because you are muting all the strings with your fretting hand.

Next, strum a guitar by using only down-strums along with the metronome click, or in other words, use one down-strum on every beat/click. Try to strum all strings at first.

Here is how the exercise looks when written down (Ex 1):

Tempo: 60 bpm

1	2	3	4	1	2	3	4 ....
D	D	D	D	D	D	D	D ....

D - down-strum, or a downstroke

1,2,3,4 - first, second, third and fourth beat in one bar (because of 4/4 time, remember?). Each beat is represented with its respective number.

This is counted as: *one...two...three...four...* at an even tempo along with the metronome click. After the 'four', the count starts from one again (new bar, and it goes on and on).

You should count the numbers out loud when you are first starting out with this exercise. Also, always try to tap your left foot (if you're right handed) along with the beat. It will help you get synced with it.

2. As you get comfortable playing equally on the beat, raise the speed of the metronome to 80 bpm and do the same. When you play like this (one strum per beat), you're playing **quarter notes** (in rhythm language).

Make sure that you raise the speed only when you feel really comfortable playing at the current one.

By being comfortable I mean: you can keep the beat for a fair amount of time (30 seconds at least), your pick doesn't slip or falls out of your hand, and you're not getting tired too much.

3. Raise the speed to 100 bpm and do the same. Then go to 120 bpm. Notice that at 120 bpm you are playing twice as fast than when you first started. Make sure that you are synced in with the metronome, let your whole body feel and move with the beat.

4. After a couple of minutes of doing this, revert the metronome back to 60 bpm and try to use 2 down-strums for every beat. You're now playing at the same speed as you did on 120 bpm, but you're playing **two notes per one beat**. These are now called **eight notes** because we've just subdivided the beat in two.

- Here's how it looks like written down (Ex 2):

Tempo: 60 bpm

```
1   +   2   +   3   +   4   +   1   +   2   +   3   +   4   +
D   D   D   D   D   D   D  ...........................
```

Pluses (+) here are units of time between the beats. They divide the beat and are counted as "*and*".

You need to count this out loud like this: *one and two and three and four and one and two and three and four and...* etc, when you practice.

5. After you get comfortable, raise the speed to 80 bpm and play the eight notes again. You might notice that it's getting tiring and uncomfortable. Since you're using all down-strums it gets really hard to keep the pace.

6. Raise the speed to 100 bpm, and after that to 120 bpm with 2 notes (two down-strums) per beat. This might be really hard, but as you play faster and faster **you don't have to down-strum all strings, just the thickest E to D** (at these speeds you're actually playing common rock rhythm). Notice that you're now playing 4 times faster than when you first started with quarter notes on 60 bpm.

Strumming exercise part 2 - Introducing up-strums

7. Now it's time to introduce the up-strums (or upstrokes if you will). Many people assume that they need to up-strum all guitar strings, but this is not the case in real playing.

On your up-strum it's enough to hit only the bottom 3-4 strings (high e to G or D strings).

Go back to 60 bpm and play one note per beat. Then add the up-strum (or an upstroke) between the beats. Make sure that every down-strum falls on the beat, and that every up-strum is between the beats (when your foot goes up). Also make sure that your strumming hand is moving down and up continuously in a natural and relaxed way, as described many times before.

- (Ex 3):

Tempo: 60 bpm

```
1   +   2   +   3   +   4   +   1   +   2   +   3   +   4   +
D   U   D   U   D   U   D   U   D.....................
```

U - up-strum or an upstroke

It's counted the same way as in Ex 2.

8. Do the same thing by raising the tempos as explained: 60-80-100-120 bpm. As you get to 120 bpm you'll start noticing that it's a very different, less energetic and more smoother feeling than when you used all down strums. Using the up strums 'softens' the rhythm a lot and makes it much easier to play at the higher speeds.

Strumming exercise part 3 - 16th note strumming

9. Once you feel comfortable playing eight notes at 120 bpm (down-strum on the beat and up-strum in between), go back to 60 bpm again. Now we're going to subdivide the beat in four. This is where it gets rough! :)

Instead of playing down on the beat and up in between, you're now going to play down once on a beat, then: up-down-up. To divide the beat in four we use phonetics: 'ee' and 'ah'.

- Here is how it looks like written down (Ex 4):

Tempo: 60 bpm

```
1  e  +  a  2  e  +  a  3  e  +  a  4  e  +  a  ....
D  U  D  U  D  U  D  U  D  U  D  U  D  U  D  U  ....
```

'e' - a unit of time between the beat and the 'and'

'a' - a unit of time between the 'and' and the beat

The count is: *one ee and ah two ee and ah three ee and ah four ee and ah*, etc.

   I might be repeating myself a lot, but it is very important that your hand needs to keep moving all the time so that you're on the beat. If you learn to **feel** the beat first you will move your body with it naturally. That is why a metronome is an essential part of this exercise - because it keeps you in check. You are learning how to play on the beat and keep time.

   Playing **4 notes per one beat** in a bar of four beats (4/4 time) means that you're playing **sixteenth notes**. You should get used to playing sixteenth notes at 60 bpm, and practice on that speed for a while.

10. Raise the speed to 80-100-120 bpm. Make sure that you get used to comfortably keeping the beat while strumming on each of these tempos.

   Once you hit 120 bpm, and are comfortable with that speed, I can only say congratulations! :) That is more than enough for general playing. You can raise the speed even further then, especially if you want to move into styles like funk and RnB, or metal. You can also practice gallops or triplets used quite often in metal music.

   In any case, after doing this exercise for a few minutes (to the point where it becomes challenging) try to strum some chords and you'll instantly feel a big difference in the feel and the consistency of your strumming. This is one of the best strumming exercises that will do wonders to your strumming technique. But please keep in mind that at first you might not be able to complete the whole exercise!

It is very important that you practice slowly at first and just push yourself just a little bit beyond your comfort zone every time.

If you find that playing eight notes at 80 bpm causes you to make too many mistakes, you should work on that speed for a while or even revert back on speed a little bit. You need to become comfortable playing on that speed at first before moving on.

Sixteenth notes at 120 bpm is the highest speed where I can strum and be somewhat comfortable, anything above that and I start getting tired and making mistakes. If you can strum faster than me make sure to let me know. ;)

The great thing is - this is just a starting point. You can modify this exercise as much as you want in any way that you wish, and incorporate chords and different rhythms and techniques.

One can explain you in detail how to strum, but you will only learn it when you actually do it. It's like learning to ride a bike.

6 strumming patterns

Now it's time to introduce the basic strumming patterns. A strumming pattern is a pattern by which your strumming hand hits (strums) the strings, while moving down and up continuously. It's what makes simple chord strumming more musical and interesting. The patterns I'm going to show you are widely used in songs, but some are made to be more difficult on purpose because they serve as a great exercise. Playing only down and up consecutively can get overdone and boring really fast, so we're going to spice up your strumming with some new strumming patterns and techniques.

I'll use D - down-strum and U - up-strum again to show you the new patterns.

The numbers below are the numbers of the beat. They show where the beat is in a bar and represent the metronome click. I've already explained what "and" or "+" is.

All of the strumming patterns below are in 4/4 time with an eight note feel. We'll leave 16th note strumming patterns for another time.

When you try these patterns remember that the beat will always be a down-strum, and "and" or "+" is always an up-strum because we're playing eight notes. This might not necessarily always be the case because for some songs (usually of reggae genre) it's better to use down-strums on the "and's", depending on the feel and the groove of a song. It's a good idea to experiment with this after you master the basics.

You can practice this patterns with any chord but I recommend that you start with E major. It's a nice full sounding open chord. Your strumming hand is going to do all of the work here.

You'll also need to use a metronome again. It's easy to lose time when you're playing patterns (especially the tougher ones), that's why metronome is there to make sure you're on time. In the next section we'll see exactly why is it so important to use a metronome.

For all these patterns set the metronome to 60 bpm. Speed is not important here. What's important is that you play evenly, keep the time, and that it sounds good.

- *Strumming pattern #1*

D		D	U	D		D	U
1		2	+	3		4	+

This is an easy one.

The count is: "one, two and three, four and", then you go back from the top again. You can say this out loud and play the pattern by clapping your hands.

In terms of the actual strumming, it goes like this: down, down-up-down, down-up; but making sure that the down-strum is on the beat at an even tempo along with the metronome click. Also make sure that the chord is sounding nice and clear.

- *Strumming pattern #2*

D	U	D		D		D	U
1	+	2		3		4	+

Can you do the count for this one? You can figure it out easily on your own by watching the previous example.

It's another very common strumming pattern. As a bonus, you can try combining the two patterns - play the Ex 1 pattern for one bar, and then for the second bar play the Ex 2 pattern. This is just another thing you can do that will help your strumming.

- Strumming pattern #3

D		D	U		U	D	U
1		2	+	(3)	+	4	+

This pattern is more challenging than the first two because it requires that you miss the down-strum on the 3rd beat. That's why the 3rd beat is in parenthesis.

Count: "one, two and ... and four and"

When you count this you can whisper the beat that is not being played. In this case three.

Strumming goes like this: down, down-up, up-down-up.

Remember when I said that your strumming hand needs to be moving continuously down and up? Rhetorical question, but this is the reason why. In order to play this pattern while keeping time and staying on the beat, you hand needs to be moving all the time. When you get to the 3rd beat your hand must not stop. You just move it down across the strings but miss them completely and don't play anything. As your hand goes back up it hits the strings again. Hope you get the idea. :)

This is probably the most commonly used strumming pattern that you'll ever learn. It just takes some time to get used to.

Strumming pattern #4

D	U		U		U	D	U
1	+	(2)	+	(3)	+	4	+

This pattern misses two beats instead of just one. It's not as common as the 3rd one but still pretty useful nonetheless.

Count: "one and ... and ... and four and"

Strumming: down-up, up, up, up-down-up

Strumming pattern #5

D	U	D		D	U	D
1	+	2		3	+	4

Pretty straightforward. I'll let you do the count and figure out the strumming for this one. Note that here we finish our bar on beat 4 rather than on the "and" after the 4 as in the previous examples.

Strumming pattern #6

	U		U		U	D	U
(1)	+	(2)	+	(3)	+	4	+

Out of all the patterns so far this is the hardest one because the strongest beat in a bar (1) is not played. This is very rarely used in songs, but you should practice this anyway because it will improve your feel and your rhythm skills tremendously. It forces you to really pay attention, feel where the beat is, and know what you're doing.

Count: "... and ... and ... and four and"

Strumming: up, up, up, up-down-up

As metronome clicks, your strumming hand strums down but without hitting any of the strings (missed beat), and then you hit the strings on an upstroke ("+"). On the next down-stroke (2nd beat) you miss the strings again and play the following upstroke ("+"). Repeat this again for the 3rd beat and finish with a down-up ("4 +").

You're going to struggle with this pattern but it will be worth it!

These patterns will keep you busy for awhile and they will allow you to play many songs and get the feel for strumming, rhythm and timing. Knowing these will also allow you to experiment with your own strumming patterns - which is very easy to do.

Simply write down beats like this: "1 + 2 + 3 + 4 +", and then add the Downs (D) and Ups (U) anywhere you want.

For example, you can play a down-strum (D) on the "1" and on the last "+" (U) that goes after the 4th beat. Try doing that for a challenge. ;) Experiment and make it as hard or as easy as you want.

Another thing you might want to try is to lower the speed(?!) Yes, lowering the speed of a metronome will make the strumming pattern exercises much harder because the emphasis will be on your timing and less on your strumming technique. On higher speeds you're working more on your technique.

For lower speeds (below 60 bpm) you really need to feel where the beat is, and lock it in your playing. When you can do this correctly your timing will improve a lot.

After learning these patterns/exercises and adding a couple of your own patterns, lower the speed of the metronome from 60 to 50 bpm, and then to 40 bpm. Practice these everyday for 5-10 minutes, and after some time when you get good at these, you will see great benefits in your playing.

Trust me when I say that playing these at 40 bpm and locking on the beat is very, very hard! But always remember the saying: "The harder it is, the greater the reward!"

Why you should use metronome in your practice

We've already discussed how metronome can be very beneficial to you sounding like a professional, but many new and intermediate players avoid it if they can (I know some piano players who hate it). The excuse is that practicing with a metronome is hard and frustrating, and it can make you sound robotic and stale.

I'm going to address these two excuses. First, I'm going to repeat the saying:

"The harder it is, the greater the reward!"

This is especially true for learning guitar. It might be hard and frustrating to get used to practicing with a metronome, but that goes with any new skill that you learn. Putting in the effort here will pay off.

Think about it, what gets people moving, clapping their hands and dancing at concerts, in clubs, or at home while listening to music?

- It is the groove/rhythm.

And what makes up a good rhythm?

- It's the timing, the ability to keep the beat.

The thing is, many of us are not born with the amazing musical, rhythm and timing skills. How do we learn then to keep time and develop our rhythm techniques if we're not talented?

- Practicing with a metronome helps us with this.

The more you practice keeping time with a metronome, the more that evenly spaced 'click' sound is going to become internalized, allowing you to keep the beat while playing. It will be felt in your playing when you're performing in front of an audience, while listening to your recordings, or when you're playing just for yourself without the metronome.

It's better to mess up the chords while playing than to mess up your rhythm or timing. As long you stay on time and keep the beat and the groove going, making it interesting, messing up the chords won't matter much. If you mess up your strumming and fall out of time, it's going to sound bad and unskillful. Simple as that.

Another very common excuse is that metronome can make you sound robotic, aka boring, without any emotion or a feel in your playing. This is simply not true.

It's not the metronome that makes you sound this way, it's the lack of the rhythm skills like:

- playing with dynamics (playing loud, soft, hard, quiet...),

- using accents (accenting certain beats and imitating the snare drums),

- build-ups (building up rhythms)

- chord muting (a technique used a lot in chord strumming)

- syncopation (playing primarily on the off-beats)

- using triplets (like gallops in metal, but also used in genres like jazz)

- tempo changes (playing certain parts of the song faster or slower, but at an even pace)

- variety of strumming patterns (and the ability to make up your own while playing)

- phrasing (the way in which you phrase a note, a chord, a solo... It's really a mix of your feel and all your rhythm skills combined. For exceptional phrasing take a listen to Joe Satriani and songs like Cryin', Love Thing, Surfing with the Alien...

Explaining all these skills is going to require a whole course, dedicated only to developing great rhythm skills. Stay tuned for that.

So yes, practicing with a metronome is important. It's what almost all professional musicians have done, and are doing still from time to time. I would advise you to use a metronome every time you're working on your technique, if you can, but also make sure that you're playing lots of songs and recording yourself so that you can check how your time and sound improves over time.

More ways to develop great rhythm

There are better ways to practice your timing than with a metronome. You might be wondering why I haven't mentioned those by now, but the simple reason is that they are not the most convenient, or available options for everybody. These are not the alternatives, but rather additions to the metronome.

I'm talking about the drum machines and playing/jamming with a drummer, or other much more experienced guitar players.

Drum machines are basically electronic drums in the form of a device/machine, or a computer software. They are used in electronic music. You can use a drum machine to play with a real sounding drums rather than with a simple metronome click. It is more fun and real at the same time. Drum machines have a bit of a learning curve before you can use them effectively and program your own drums in any way that you like.

Another way you can develop your timing and rhythm techniques is by practicing and playing with a drummer. It is way more fun and it puts you in real playing conditions. This is the best way to learn in my opinion.

The problem is, as I've said, not everybody has a buddy who can play drums well enough, or who is a much more experienced guitar player with whom you can jam (jam - playing instruments in a group of at least two people and having fun) and pick tricks from.

Luckily (unless you live on a remote desert island) you'll be able to find people to jam with relatively easy. Go to your local music store and ask if they can recommend a group or someone specific. Some music stores have ad boards with players looking for players to jam with. Also check local music forums online, local groups, music schools or even post your own ads. If you have a guitar teacher, you can also ask him to recommend something.

If you really try hard enough you will meet new people, make new contacts, and eventually you'll find someone and maybe even form a band. Possibilities are great!

Keep in mind though that you might still need to use the metronome just because it's very practical and accessible anytime you want.

Where to next?

The material covered in this book is meant to give you the basics for setting you up on your path toward guitar mastery. It's going to take you at least a couple of months (depending on your practice regime) to fully absorb, comprehend and learn this material.

We've covered a lot of ground here: buying guitar, mindset, note circle, reading tabs, theory, basic chords, exercises, strumming... We've touched some basics of the music theory and its application on guitar.

There are many routes that you can take from here, but the wisest thing to do would be to continue working on the basics, until my next book comes out. ;)

By 'basics' I mean:

- Being able to play different 8th and 16th note patterns and make up your own 'on the spot'.

- understanding basic music theory: how scales are made, how to use them, how to solo/improvise, how chords are constructed, chord types, concept of the root note, intervals, CAGED system.

- understanding and being able to play the open chords (plus their variations and inversions) and barre chords, and how to move them around a guitar neck...

- being able to learn songs by ear - recognize strumming patterns instantly and quickly find the chords that you hear in a song. This is also called transcribing.

- make up your own arrangements of the songs.

There is a lot of stuff here, and everything will be covered in the series of books that I'm making. So stay tuned.

Guitar players often label themselves in terms of their skill levels on: beginners, intermediates, advanced, professionals, legends, gods etc. In my opinion, and even though I don't to like to use this labels at all, if you know all the basics, then you're an advanced guitar player. It would be a good idea then to further specialize your skills in a particular area or a style that interests you the most - like rock, blues or metal for example. By the way, since we're using labels, being called 'professional guitar player' means that you're making money playing guitar, no matter what your skill level is.

Conclusion

I want to sincerely thank you for purchasing this book and I really hope that you got an amazing value from it. I've put a lot of work in this book with the purpose of sharing what I know and helping you learn guitar.

If you feel that this book helped you in any way and you want to say thank you, please consider writing an honest review on Amazon. It will help a lot.

The link above will take you straight to the review page for this book. It helps other people find it, and it encourages me as well to create more awesome content for you. Also please share this book with anyone that you think might benefit from it.

Don't forget that you will learn this instrument only if you take action: practice, get inspired, play, improvise, jam, keep a positive view... All the work that you put in will pay off, you just have to stick with it and learn to enjoy the process; and in no time you'll find yourself playing your favorite songs on guitar!

Wishing you all the best,
Nicolas Knoll

Check out my other books

- Kaizen: *The Art of Continuous Life Improvement, How to Create a Lasting Change One Step at a Time*

goo.gl/CMm2bD

As the title suggests, this book is all about the ways you can the art of Kaizen to improve your everyday life and achieve significant goals.

- Meditation for Beginners: *7 Incredible and Easy Ways to Still Your Mind, Hear the Voice of your Intuition and Trust Your Heart through Meditation*

goo.gl/xgakeR

You might be wondering what meditation and playing guitar have in common?! Well, playing guitar is a meditation in its own way. Learning how to meditate allows you to look within yourself, get inspired again and set your priorities, amongst many other things. Meditation helps your mindset in a way that it makes it impossible to fail, if you just learn how to follow your heart! If learning how to play a guitar is what you truly want, then meditation can really help you with that.

Printed in Germany
by Amazon Distribution
GmbH, Leipzig